THE FACE OF DIGITAL

How Digital Technologies Are Changing
The $565 Billion Dollar Events Industry

THE
FACE OF
DIGITAL

INSIDE THE ORIGINAL SOCIAL NETWORKS

MARCO GIBERTI AND **JAY WEINTRAUB**

THE FACE OF DIGITAL

How Digital Technologies Are Transforming the $565 Billion Dollar Events Industry

ISBN   978-1-61961-647-9 *Paperback*

978-1-61961-648-6 *Ebook*

CONTENTS

——

PROLOGUE: MARCO 9

PROLOGUE: JAY 15

INTRODUCTION 19

1. THE FEAR IN THE AIR 51

2. TECTONIC FORCES AT PLAY 71

3. LESSONS FROM OTHER INDUSTRIES.... 113

4. MAGICAL OPPORTUNITIES 133

CONCLUSION 147

APPENDIX: SUPPORTING DATA 157

ABOUT THE AUTHORS........................ 185

PROLOGUE: MARCO

As I write this prologue, I'm in the waiting area of the airport in San Luis Potosí, a remote city in the center of Mexico. I'm returning to the United States after giving a presentation on the past, present, and future of the events industry at the Latin American and Mexican Event Organizers Conference. Most of the presentation, and the ensuing question-and-answer session, were dedicated to discussing the influence of digital innovation on the face-to-face events industry.

Last week, I was in Nashville, where I was part of a similar panel for the world's largest experiential marketing company. A couple of months ago, I addressed the same topic for the World Trade Show association. The list goes on.

The appetite for understanding digital technologies and their impact on face-to-face events is huge and growing. While many other industries have had their moment of digital disruption, events are still in the early phase of transformation. This is an exciting development. At the same time, however, people are terrified of the changes digital technology may create and the corresponding imperative to adapt.

Thousands of event-tech and marketing-tech companies are launching at the intersection of face-to-face events and digital. The pace of change is electric, and now is the time to learn from transitions in other industries. What can we learn from publishing, for example, that will help us rejuvenate the face-to-face industry without major pain?

I've worked in media, tech, and events for more than 25 years. I started as a marketer with Apple, a role that brought me into contact with events from the perspective of a corporation using them as a marketing tool. After that, I moved into producing and organizing events, and grew to understand the challenges faced by organizers with a responsibility for connecting exhibitors, sponsors, and visitors.

Since then, I've been a company cofounder, a board member, and an investor in event- and marketing-tech companies. I recognize the concerns of exhibitors and sponsors who are sick of paying thousands of dollars for positions at events without being able to measure their returns on investment. I know that visitors are frustrated when they attend seventy-thousand-person events without knowing in advance whom they should meet. I understand the pain experienced by all these groups of people, which is what makes me so excited by the potential of technology to address it.

The changes I've seen during the past couple of years have been more dramatic than those I've witnessed during the previous two decades, and I'm convinced that this is only the beginning. I suspect that the next five to ten years will redefine the way that we think of digital media in connection with live events. That's why this book exists.

As an entrepreneur, I love building things from scratch, exploring ideas that seem crazy, and fixing problems in need of a solution. Since my early days with Apple, I've always been excited by the transformations taking place at the cutting edge and the people who spearhead those ideas with such determination. It wasn't until I met Jay Weintraub, however, and we realized that we share an understanding of the state of the industry, that I found the perfect partner in crime with whom to write this book.

Jay is an exceptionally smart entrepreneur who understands tech and events in a way that few people within either industry do. It has been a true pleasure brainstorming the ideas in this book with him. We have already learned so many valuable lessons about how technology is shaping the live events industry, and yet there are so many more lessons to learn.

In many ways, this book is a selfish endeavor. It has given me an excuse to talk to smart people in the live events industry and engage in fascinating conversations about the potential challenges, threats, and opportunities that digital technology is bringing to live events. The book is not a collection of solutions. It's too early for that. The industry is still very much in flux, and I have no doubt that many of the most powerful shifts are yet to take place. Instead, it's a snapshot of an industry in the process of change and an attempt to understand what happens next.

Much of the content in these pages focuses on trade shows, but, in fact, the potential impact is much broader. Every kind of live event, from concerts and sporting events to conferences, will be affected. Whatever your niche, there is value for you in exploring the potential of digital technology to improve your business.

Jay and I are not gurus or futurologists. We want to share our own experiences, mistakes, and lessons with you, so that we can all benefit. This book draws on those experiences, and also on the experiences of some of the savviest and most successful leaders in the events industry, along with some of the most farsighted and adventurous entrepreneurs disrupting the space.

We want to start a conversation, not finish one. We value debate and intellectual challenge because we all grow from listening to one another and exploring questions together. Almost every day, I see an innovation that could make a considerable difference in the industry if it is built and marketed in the right way. Nonetheless, there are some common denominators. Most of the people Jay and I have spoken to agree that the events industry is not ripe for a huge disruption, in the mold of Uber or Airbnb. Instead, it's more likely that hundreds, even thousands, of small players will emerge to solve individual problems.

If you're an event organizer, a marketer, or a C-level corporate executive who invests time and money in live events, you will surely want to know how you can take advantage of this movement. How can you keep adding technology into your marketing mix? How can you make events more relevant and sustainable throughout the year? How can you build a digital conversation that complements the face-to-face one, instead of obscuring it? I hope you'll ask yourself these questions and more as you read.

I also hope that you enjoy reading this book as much as I enjoyed writing it and talking with all those amazing people. I thank each of them enormously for their time and for the invaluable knowledge they have shared during our meetings, dinners, coffees, and long conversations.

PROLOGUE: JAY

———

Millions of people engage with individual events every day, just as millions of people engage with retail establishments. Few people, however, think of their local florist as part of a global retail community. By the same token, I'd guess that hardly any of the people who attend events think of them as part of an interconnected industry, with shared priorities and challenges.

Nonetheless, that's what they are. Each retail store is a single node in a much larger system, and each event is a data point on a far greater map. Even the largest individual retail brands constitute a negligible percentage of total retail sales, and the same is true of the largest events.

Platforms such as Facebook and Google are centralized, so people naturally think of them as foundations on which to build a vast range of businesses. The events industry lacks this kind of centralization, making it wonderfully diverse and enthralling, yet also comparatively fragmented.

During times of stability, incumbent players can judge the health of an ecosystem. In the case of events, those players may ask whether there are a lot of shows, whether the shows are growing, and whether delegate numbers are up. In times of transformation, however, the only way to judge an ecosystem's health is to observe the levels of innovation.

At the time of writing, digital transformation is knocking hard on the doors of trade shows. We can answer the door and welcome it in, or we can put our fingers in our ears and pretend we don't hear. Either way, such transformation will make an entrance. The only question is whether we make it our friend and harness it to make our lives better, or let it chart its own, potentially damaging, course through the industry.

Two decades ago, few people would have predicted the deep impact digital technology has had on the retail or newspaper industries. By treating digital innovation largely as a necessary evil, however, both these sectors have suffered. We don't want to see the same thing happen in the events space.

There is a better way. Some of the events Marco and I get involved in are insurance conferences. The insurance industry is very interesting, in relation to this book, because it nurtures a lot of the things I'd like to see in the events industry. There are accelerators dedicated purely to insurance innovation. There are ventures focused on driving fresh developments. These are signs of an industry that has understood the risk of disruption and chosen instead to participate actively in choosing a path.

I started in events because I attended a show and had an idea. I was a domain expert in a particular form of digital. I'd been to a handful of shows, but I thought of them as nothing more complex than places where my colleagues gathered. I had no sense of Comic Con, an NBA game, and a Formula One race all being part of the same family. I was looking for a place to do business and share knowledge. I realized that there wasn't one, and moved toward events because I couldn't think of a better vehicle for bringing about the kind of sharing that I think is valuable for the community.

On the surface, this book speaks to the transformation taking place in the events ecosystem. My real hope, however, is that the book will act not only as a catalog of innovation, but also as a spur to further innovation. It is an attempt, by two people who have drunk the Kool-Aid, to encourage more people to embrace the awesome power of face-to-face events and play a part in their evolution. We want to ensure the vibrancy of the ecosystem we call home. In that sense, this is a self-serving project. We love this industry and want it to continue thriving, so that we can continue to be part of it.

Like an event, you can take several routes through these pages. The book can be read from cover to cover, but is also designed to allow you to dip in wherever you like. Consume it however you choose, whether that's through focusing on a particular area or taking a journey from page one to the back cover.

We discuss some potentially scary developments, but we're not trying to create panic. Quite the reverse, in fact: we want to highlight how amazing this industry is and to make the case for the innovation that will allow it to become even more amazing in years to come.

INTRODUCTION

A TRANSFORMATIVE EXPERIENCE

———

Change happens in an instant, but it takes a long time to arrive.

There's a fascinating YouTube video of a fox that is hunting in the snow.[1] The fox spends what seems like an eternity exploring the landscape, sniffing, observing, and triangulating. It makes several failed attempts to secure a meal.

Suddenly, the fox pounces and emerges with its prey. The movement happens in a split second, and, to the animal that becomes the fox's dinner, it is an enormous surprise.

1   https://www.youtube.com/watch?v=D2S0GHFM18I

The time spent in preparation and experimentation, however, is essential.

Innovation takes a similar route. Sometimes it's difficult to see progress. The path is littered with failed attempts. Then, an abrupt shift takes place and an industry's center of gravity shifts.

This is what we believe is happening as the events industry encounters the incredible potential of the digital world. It's not yet clear when the fox will spring out of nowhere, galvanizing changes that will ripple through the entire field. What *is* clear is that the fox is on the prowl.

Ultimately, the impact of digital technology will be a net positive for the industry. It will make events better and open up previously unimaginable possibilities. It will drive necessary investment in digital technologies. Like all change, however, it will be painful at first, especially for those who don't see it coming.

To those who understand the direction the industry is taking, the leap will be a smooth one. It will feel like being that fox, reaping the benefits of many hours of preparation and many unsuccessful attempts to catch the zeitgeist. Those who don't see it coming will feel like the fox's prey, trapped by something shocking and unexpected.

In the words of Brian Casey, president of the Center for Exhibition Industry Research (CEIR), and David DuBois, president and CEO of the International Association of Exhibitions and Events (IAEE): "Tech is a disruptor, and those who are going to be successful in the future need to embrace change."

THE OLDEST MARKETING TOOL IN THE WORLD

Arguably, meeting people face-to-face is the oldest marketing tool in the world. Trade shows and fairs have existed for at least 850 years, and in all that time, there has been very little disruption or innovation within the industry.

The blueprint has remained essentially the same: people meet, interact, do business together, and go home. Today, however, digital technology is influencing all aspects of business, and the events industry is finally beginning to feel the impact.

We, your authors, regularly present at conferences aimed at senior management, marketers, and event organizers. Our subject is the past, present, and future of the events industry. Specifically, we focus on digital technology and how it's altering the events industry.

At one of these conferences, a successful entrepreneur with more than thirty-five years' experience in the face-to-face events industry approached us. "I'm fascinated to learn about all these new opportunities for our industry," he told us. "I'm also terrified."

He's not alone. Many people who have been running successful and profitable events for decades are realizing that digital technologies have the potential to disrupt, or even supersede, their current operations. Conferences, trade shows, festivals, concerts, and sporting events are all vulnerable to change.

Nonetheless, the greatest source of fear and anxiety for people in the industry is not change itself but the *uncertainty* that comes with not knowing exactly how that change will manifest and, therefore, how to prepare for it. People understand that technology is disrupting the face-to-face industry, but they're not sure how fast, dramatic, and deep the shifts will ultimately prove.

Digital innovation is reshaping every sphere of our lives. In the past fifteen years, we have witnessed the radical disruption of almost every industry, beginning with traditional media's transformation to digital. Centuries-old institutions have seen their core businesses decimated. The same disruption has occurred in the hospitality industry, travel sector, music, movies, and broadcast TV, along with unlikely areas such as taxi service.

Face-to-face events, by comparison, have undergone relatively few changes. Digital will affect the face-to-face industry. There are already signs that change is coming. The only questions are "How?" and "When?"

Consider the paid search industry. In 1996, there was no such thing as paid search. Ten years later, it was an $8 billion industry showing no signs of slowing down. Technology altered the industry so much that it created an entirely new job title, the paid search manager. Imagine, however, what it must have been like to be involved in paid search in its early years, before it was even a product and long before it became an "always on" advertising channel.

We were there. It was an exciting, yet nerve-wracking, experience. In the beginning, it was unclear whether this nascent industry would blossom and become self-sustaining, or whether it would go the way of many other promising ideas. For those early digital pioneers, however, the question was never what impact paid search would have on incumbent channels. They had discovered a new way to reach people, and figuring out how to make the most of it was all that mattered.

In 2017, events and event tech are in a similar phase. There is clear potential, and also an understanding that digital innovation will almost certainly alter the industry considerably over the coming decade. There is also a great deal of uncertainty. No one knows exactly *which* innovations will break through and become successful and which will fall by the wayside. As was the case with paid search, the majority of those at the forefront of innovation are focused purely on what they perceive as an opportunity to solve an existing problem. They aren't thinking about the broader impact of their discoveries. Only those of us who have seen this movie before are both excited and worried.

Your authors have personally invested time and money in companies with big ideas at the junction of events and technology. Some of those companies are thriving, and some have fallen at the first hurdle. In this book, we'll be sharing both the lessons we've learned from our activities and the insights and opinions of respected figures in the fields of events and technology.

You may have heard about businesses whose founders are asked about their overnight successes and respond by explaining that what appears to be an overnight success actually has its roots in years of work. Steve Jobs said as much about many of Apple's major coups. They may have looked like moments of inspiration, but they were based on years of research, development, and testing.

This is the kind of change we see coming to the face-to-face industry. As more sophisticated entrepreneurs and investors begin to approach event tech from different angles, changes that look instantaneous, but have actually been years in the making, will rise to the surface.

This is an incredibly exciting time. Your authors love both events and technology, and find it extremely inspiring to see them intersecting in a way that will forever change the world of events.

WHY ARE EVENTS STILL RELEVANT?

Despite the massive changes sweeping the digital world and the ubiquity of smartphones, in-person events remain the most effective marketing channel for a broad range of industries.

For this reason, most at-scale businesses allocate a healthy percentage of their marketing budgets to organizing and promoting face-to-face events. Moreover, these budgets continue to grow, which is why trade shows, product launches, conferences, festivals, concerts, sporting events, and gatherings comprise an industry with an annual turnover of half a trillion dollars.

The media landscape has fragmented since the advent of digital. Arguably, so too has the face-to-face industry.

Take trade shows, for example. Not long ago, they were the only game in town for many businesses who wanted to meet clients and prospects face-to-face, or to showcase new iterations of their products. Although trade shows are still one of the largest single segments of the face-to-face ecosystem, and continue to attract large expenditures of marketing dollars, they are no longer the only option, and for some companies they are no longer the default option.

Today, smaller niche and corporate events are becoming both more common and more attractive. The Consumer Electronics Show (CES) remains one of the largest events in the industry, but numerous companies, such as Microsoft, Google, Facebook, and Salesforce, are now holding their own events aimed at very specific segments of the population.

While each industry has its own de facto meeting place, more and more are seeking not only to participate in larger industry events but also to create their *own* events. In some cases, these have become the new industry standard: for example, Salesforce's Dreamforce in the customer relationship management (CRM) space. The fox may very well be on the prowl.

Although most companies haven't pulled out of large trade shows, some have. Apple is perhaps the most obvious example. The company no longer attends CES but continues to run its own face-to-face events, hyperfocused on new Apple products. Facebook, too, is a company with a huge focus on the digital world but a clear commitment to creating in-person events.

Money continues to flow into face-to-face events because they represent a form of value that is not easily replaced. In a technological world, relationships forged in person continue to differ qualitatively from those formed online. In a world of infinite "likes," meeting people creates a connection that no amount of interaction on social media can match.

Polish sociologist Zygmunt Bauman tells a story about an acquaintance boasting of making five hundred Facebook friends in a single day. Bauman responds that in eighty-six years, he has not succeeded in making that many friends. "Presumably," Bauman continues, "we don't mean the same thing. It's a different kind of friend."[2]

You may have five hundred Facebook friends, or even five thousand, but what impact does that really have on your business? Do their status updates have a significant impact on the way you feel about them or their businesses? Would you refer business to them or recommend their

---

2   https://www.youtube.com/watch?v=LcHTeDNIarU

services? Now imagine that you have met them all face-to-face and shared an experience with them. Would their updates carry more weight and hold greater meaning if you knew them personally?

This is why in-person events continue to be relevant, and why they will remain relevant for the foreseeable future. The human need for face-to-face interaction is instinctual and fundamental. It is the basis of trust, and we all feel better about doing business with people we trust. We may behave like *Homo digitalis* for most of our waking hours, but we cannot completely transcend our analog roots. Even as babies, we display a preference for looking at faces over other stimuli.

In the words of DoubleDutch CEO Lawrence Coburn:

> Events have long been a unique accelerator in the marketer's tool kit. No other channel can match an event's ability to push an attendee through a funnel. When you walk into an event that is buzzing, where the content is perfect, the companies the best in their category, and the attendees ideal, you know it. There is an electric energy, and this energy drives positive business outcome. This is why events command the largest chunk of the marketing spend, even with metrics and reporting that are from the Stone Age.

There may come a time when this is no longer true, and we succeed completely in overriding the neurology that makes face-to-face connection especially appealing for us. Until that time, meeting other people will continue to exert a unique pull on us.

Virtual reality (VR) and augmented reality (AR), which is sometimes known as mixed reality (MR), will continue to evolve, but we don't believe that humans are on the verge of disappearing entirely into a virtual world. Connecting directly with other people makes our lives meaningful and, from a business perspective, drives sales and revenue. The desire to purchase from people we like is often more powerful than any number of features and benefits.

Events create a context for relationships, bridging the gap between social interaction and naked commerce. They provide a forum in which brands become humanized, and people become part of a brand experience.

This is a key point. While technology will undoubtedly shift the landscape of events, it won't make them obsolete. We bond in person, and no app can change that. The technology that works in the events industry will be technology that makes it *easier* to connect with other people, not technology that replaces the human element.

The very largest and most successful tech companies, those that have pioneered digital connectivity, all rely on events to build their own brands. For Apple, Facebook, and Google, the face-to-face event is almost a rite of passage. As the site of countless giant technological leaps forward, the Apple product launch has acquired near-legendary status. The biggest tech brands are all about digital innovation, but that doesn't mean they overlook the thrill that comes from being able to say, "I was there."

TECHNOLOGY WILL REFRESH AND IMPROVE EVENTS, NOT REPLACE THEM

If you owned a mobile phone in 2005, you will recall the extraordinary popularity of BlackBerry devices. At the time, they seemed destined to rule the mobile phone market.

What happened next? The iPhone. Suddenly, the Black-Berry was no longer an indispensable accessory. At the time of writing, BlackBerry holds a market share of just 0.1 percent.[3] The company's collapse had nothing to do with the viability of the mobile phone market as a whole. Smartphones have never been more ubiquitous. In the same way, the events market will not be

---

3   https://www.bloomberg.com/news/articles/2014-05-28/
     blackberry-market-share-to-fall-to-0-3-in-2018-idc-says

killed by the advent of new technologies; its benefits run too deep.

The phone analogy is revealing. Events may *look* different, and new players may emerge who will make better use of technological developments than current leaders in the industry, but events will continue to exist in a recognizable form. The iPhone didn't kill the market for smartphones; it transformed that market.

This is both the opportunity and the risk of digital technology. Those who harness it most effectively may not be the dominant incumbent players. As the balance of power shifts, those who fail to adapt quickly enough may become BlackBerry to someone else's Apple. The *industry* will benefit, but will you?

The key distinction here is that when the iPhone emerged, it offered users an experience that BlackBerry wasn't able or willing to compete with. That experience was sufficiently appealing to entice customers to shift their loyalties in droves, although for a time many people owned both devices. This isn't to say that Apple specifically went after BlackBerry, simply that Apple's offering was so much more tempting than BlackBerry's that the latter was soon overwhelmed.

BlackBerry, focused primarily on the business arena, may not have been aware of the extent to which it was losing its grip on the market. The iPhone grew in popularity, not through targeting company bosses, but by winning consumer business. Before long, however, Apple's determination to cater to the needs of ordinary consumers filtered through to the top levels of companies. Bosses began to favor the iPhone as well. As Apple gradually won over the hearts of users, BlackBerry's core constituency eroded and finally crumbled.

The iPhone is a good example, too, of the "consumerization" of technology. Organizers are starting to worry that consumers are arriving at their events with altered expectations that they don't know how to meet. They know that face-to-face events aren't in danger of dying altogether, but they worry that they will be overtaken by a change of market direction. Like BlackBerry, they're often still blind to the shift in customer behavior that is already driving their brand toward irrelevance.

Again, this is not simply a matter of claiming that technology will influence the experiences of people attending live events. The point is also that, as yet, there's still a great deal of uncertainty about *which* technologies will win out, and exactly how events will alter as a result. Nobody wants to be BlackBerry, but neither is anyone certain what comes next.

Consumer expectations are now playing a key role in driving technological development. Anyone involved in face-to-face events *must* understand this and seek to meet or exceed those expectations. Failure to do so represents an enormous risk. Those who miss the boat as fresh technological influences emerge may be forced to watch as their customers set sail with someone else.

This is key because technology already makes sharing and connecting so much easier than it has been in previous generations. When new developments emerge, they can be adopted at incredibly rapid speed.

In upcoming chapters, we will discuss the extent to which technological change is already visible. While it's probable that change will be incremental, it's possible that the events industry's equivalent of Uber, Netflix, or the iPhone already exists and isn't yet widely recognized. Even if that's not the case, however, what's clear is that the shape of events is already changing.

HOW ARE EVENTS CHANGING?

Mike Rusbridge, former chairman of Reed Exhibitions, the globe's largest event organizer, describes event organizers as relationship brokers. For many years, putting buyers and sellers together under one roof was sufficient to generate the proverbial "event magic." Historically, event organizers believed that "If you build it, they will come." Events were a place where buyers and sellers *could* meet.

Now, expectations have changed, and the bar has been raised. Buyers and sellers are disappointed if they don't make solid connections at an event. Once, a good event consisted of good buyers and good sellers. Now, a successful event requires good buyers, good sellers, and a great experience. Tech can drive that great experience.

Rusbridge, however, sees digital "less as a threat and more as an opportunity," believing that "the industry can reap significant benefit rather than look at this as a threat to the future." He does sound a warning note, however, saying that "Failure to adapt and adopt will have severe consequences."

According to Denzil Rankine, executive chairman of AMR International, a distinguished business strategy and growth consultancy, most event organizers are "keen, rather than ready. There is appetite but not understanding." Many see tech as "an exciting and increasingly important way of adding value to face-to-face events, but they are unsure exactly how best to go about incorporating it." Reed Exhibitions, however, is "the exception. It has invested in unified systems and common approaches."

Events used to be primarily sales fairs. People would meet and do business, and that was enough. The return on investment (ROI) was very clear. As events evolve, there's a trend toward engaging in events with high publicity value but uncertain ROI.

When Coca-Cola brings Taylor Swift to Times Square, that's a huge publicity boost, but it's hard to measure what impact it has on sales. Another example is Microsoft bringing the Xbox to the X Games. It's impossible to measure how many Xboxes Microsoft sells as a result of these strategies, but the company believes there's value in creating compelling experiences.

BMW lies somewhere between the traditional model and the impulse to provide consumers with an amazing experience. The company takes a fleet of cars from city to city to give people extraordinary test drive experiences. It's possible to measure sales that result directly from this approach, but not the ongoing brand recognition and positive feelings that may develop.

Brand perception is a difficult metric to track and influence. Nonetheless, event organizers must get used to the fact that people are coming to expect experiences that spark their emotions and give them lasting memories. Intense emotional states lead to the formation of stronger relationships, both *at* the event and *with* the event.

This is a huge culture shift. At shows populated by buyers and sellers, sponsors usually cover the costs of food and drink, which are chosen on a "just good enough" basis. As people grow to expect better experiences, the "just good enough" coffee will no longer be good enough.

As a result, the cost of hosting an event will rise, even as the ROI becomes both less certain and less measurable. For people who have been focused primarily on margins, shifting to such an unpredictable model is extremely painful.

At the time of writing, it's only fifteen years since the bursting of the first dot-com bubble. When considering the huge technological developments that have taken place since then, fifteen years seems a long time. For an industry that has existed for 850 years, a decade and a half is a blink of an eye.

The events industry weathered the rise of the Internet admirably, so it would be easy to think that little has changed and that digital technology has nothing to offer in this area. A closer look, however, reveals a different picture.

There's a growing trend, for example, for events to exist in digital form long before the in-person element commences, and to continue to run digitally well beyond the conclusion of the face-to-face experience. It's now possible to open an event months in advance, lead toward an amazing three- or four-day peak, and keep it alive well after people have returned to their daily lives.

Online communities engage year-round, extending buying cycles and sustaining connections. The best shows are still those where products are launched and buying decisions are made, but they no longer have a monopoly on those activities.

People are thinking about how they can improve the face-to-face experience at events, making it more productive and ensuring that clients connect with the people they want to. Many young event organizers are thinking about building online communities first and allowing attendees at in-person events to spring from those communities.

This means continually testing and improving offerings, piloting services, and being willing to make mistakes. As online communities become stronger and more relevant, they represent a pool of potential face-to-face clients, perfectly placed to sign up for events organized by people they already know and trust.

This connectedness is also making it possible to reduce lead times and fill events at much shorter notice. When SaaStr Annual launched, the organizers only committed to it less than three months before it opened. Despite this, the inaugural event drew one thousand people.

This used to be unthinkable. Traditionally, a high-priced event, with more than one thousand participants, required at least a year of planning and marketing. Digital connectivity and the ability to reach members of an already-engaged community, however, enabled far quicker germination.

This is the tip of the iceberg. Technology promises to generate opportunities that could never have existed prior to the digital era. One caveat is that the space will probably become very crowded, very quickly.

The ubiquity of digital technologies has already produced a new breed of event organizer. Historically, most people in the events industry fell into their profession due to a combination of expertise and a desire to serve their communities.

Today, online tools such as Meetup.com, which boasts tens of thousands of users, make organizing events seem fun and socially rewarding. People enjoy the feeling of taking a lead in their community, and the recognition they receive as a result. Meetup democratizes the organization of events, allowing those who might never have seen themselves as professional event organizers to feel that bringing people together is possible.

In addition to Meetup, Eventbrite has gained phenomenal traction and has become a market leader by taking a once-complex piece of event management and transforming it into a turnkey service. Many other new-generation ticketing and registration solutions have done the same. Eventbrite may not have invented online ticketing for events, but the company has certainly popularized it. By doing so, it has made launching and running an event possible for a whole new generation of people, the vast majority of whom are new to events.

For some events, Eventbrite has also eliminated the need to create a stand-alone web page, further reducing the amount of time and effort dedicated to organization. While we don't know the exact number, we estimate that 85 percent or more of Eventbrite pages serve as primary event websites. The question event organizers must ask themselves is whether they gain anything essential from performing tasks such as website design in-house, or whether they are better served by using external platforms.

Kevin Hartz, founder and CEO of Eventbrite, tells us that the site is currently used in more than 180 countries and plays a role in facilitating everything from cricket matches in India to cycling tours in Germany. Eventbrite makes it possible for people who previously would never have considered themselves to be event organizers to enter the industry and disrupt it. If you log into Eventbrite, you will receive suggestions of events in your local area, provided by geolocation. Until recently, these events could never have reached large audiences.

Hartz believes that technology will continue to enlarge the number of services that can be offered in conjunction with events. Coachella, for example, now offers a live streaming service. Despite such disruptions, Hartz agrees that technology will not *replace* face-to-face interactions but will enhance and complement them.

For professional event organizers, these shifts pose a number of fresh questions. As participation in events is democratized, how do organizers continue to serve their community? As the digital world becomes ever more relevant, how can they improve the experience of those who invest in attending face-to-face events? Are attendees meeting the right people, in the right places? Are they seeing content that is relevant to their businesses?

In addition, organizers face the new challenge of improving the quality of content and networking that takes place both before and after the events themselves. Modern events are no longer one-off experiences. They are part of an ecosystem that lives all year long.

THE INVESTMENT CHALLENGE

One huge barrier to change is the relative paucity of investment in event tech. The events industry, for its size, attracts relatively few entrepreneurs and even fewer event-tech entrepreneurs. The industry is healthy and bursting with potential for innovation, but innovation in event tech is not particularly well supported.

Business revolutions rely on people who are willing to fund the future. Even in the past decade, the models that allow this to take place have developed significantly. The incubator model, in particular, has fundamentally transformed entrepreneurship. Some of today's biggest companies got their starts by taking part in intensive incubation programs. Ironically, one of the reasons most commonly cited for choosing incubators is the way they accelerate relationships. Even in the tech world, the benefits of face-to-face connections are palpable.

Event tech, however, is not an especially popular destination for investment. Do events not represent an appealing opportunity for entrepreneurs? Have they not attended enough events to recognize the problems or be inspired to resolve them? The answer lies in the difficulty for those funding the future to earn revenue by manufacturing an exit. Most tech entrepreneurs dream of the big idea that will enable them to raise enormous amounts of venture capital and build a business that is acquired by one of the giants of the tech world. In the events industry, the path from innovation to exit is not well trodden.

This creates a vicious cycle. Twitter, LinkedIn, and Facebook exert an enormous amount of influence on the state of the events industry, but the events industry does not exert a reciprocal influence on Twitter, LinkedIn, and Facebook. In essence, the industry is reduced to responding reactively to shifts in technology, as opposed to driving them proactively.

Additionally, there is the question of whether using these platforms to promote events is preferable to building new, dedicated ones. Both approaches have advantages and disadvantages, but there's a risk that using existing platforms means, essentially, building someone else's business.

This situation is not set in stone. An influx of innovation dollars in event tech would raise the prospect of profitable exits, thereby encouraging more people to invest time and energy in creating technologies aimed specifically at the events industry. Technology already exists that can make face-to-face events better, but the industry hasn't yet effectively tackled the thorny question of how to build on these technologies in a way that's industry specific.

Change from within the events industry is slow, because so much of it consists of people with existing businesses. Almost by definition, these people tend toward a conservative attitude, preferring to focus on protecting their operations—for example by hitting profit-and-loss projections. Innovation is almost always a cost center, especially in the formative years.

Thus, significant change often comes from external sources, because people outside the industry are less invested in current models. They have the freedom to approach problems holistically, with fewer financial constraints, and to solve those problems for the industry as a whole, not merely for a single company.

This tension creates a challenge, with those within the industry inclined to resist change, while those external players who might be interested in catalyzing change find the environment relatively unwelcoming. Ultimately, the resolution of this tension will make the industry better. As more people within the industry recognize the inevitability of change, the willingness to embrace it will surely grow.

Investment follows investor confidence. When people believe that they will generate a profit, or that their investment will result in huge efficiencies and cost savings, they are willing to spend money. Online event registration has experienced a healthy level of investment, mostly because it is already familiar to investors from other industries. They do not need to be event experts to have experience of the transition from paper to electronic tickets, and having seen the shift take place in other markets, they can easily extrapolate to events. Other event-tech solutions and opportunities, however, are less clear. Without deep domain expertise, therefore, they are much less likely to receive support.

Not surprisingly, event owners have mostly found themselves in the role of customers, rather than innovation leaders. They have been afraid, unsure of what to build, and unwilling to invest capital in ventures with no immediate prospect of generating a return. Even successful incumbents, with plenty of available capital, have not been minded to funnel it into speculative projects that could transform the industry, but offer no guarantees. Funding the future is often a thankless job when one's own balance sheet is on the line.

This is beginning to change. For the first time in the history of the events industry, huge event organizers are showing an inclination to partner with early-stage companies and create an environment in which both can learn. They are starting to understand that unless they forge links with young entrepreneurs and disruptors, they will watch emerging trends pass them by and lose their preeminent positions in the market.

We invested in a marketing technology company, with a remit to replicate some existing marketing tech solutions and retool them for event tech. The company started with a retargeting technology that has been extremely successful in a short period. As a result, it has been able to command significant investment and grow its operations, winning incumbents not only as clients but also as investors.

While it may not be obvious to outsiders, events are part of the media industry. Obviously, everyone who is even tangentially connected with the media industry has seen the bloodbath of the last fifteen years and wondered how it might affect them. In comparison with print media, the amount of disruption in the face-to-face industry has been quite limited, but that hasn't stopped people looking over their shoulders as they see other, connected industries seriously affected.

There's a mixture of fear and skepticism in the industry, which doesn't help the investment use case. Some older event organizers are very concerned about the changes they see around them and the impact those changes could have on their business. Others have seen face-to-face events ride the digital wave for a decade or more and have concluded that this arena will never be significantly affected.

Fortunately, there is a growing subset of people within the events industry, particularly digital natives who have grown up with technological incursions into their lives, who realize that tech will eventually permeate events. These people advocate a proactive approach designed to prepare the face-to-face industry for upcoming shifts.

At the same time, some forward-thinking investors, private equity firms, and venture capitalists are showing an interest in event tech. Tracxn, an influential consulting firm, reported in January 2017 that more than $1.96 billion was invested in 2015–16, with 372 companies funded in the last five years, among 1,600-plus companies in the sector.

Tech innovators generally view the events industry with a mixture of excitement and frustration. They are enthusiastic about the size of the industry and the scale of the available business opportunities, but disheartened by the relative lack of sophistication shown by many industry players and their reluctance to embrace technological innovation.

As more millennials rise to prominence in the industry, we believe this situation will change rapidly. They have grown up with technology and embrace its use in every aspect of their lives. They understand that innovation is essential to the future of events.

Here's an example: Mobile apps have become almost ubiquitous within the events industry. Their usage stemmed from a desire to replace, or at least augment, catalogs and directories at events. The real power of an event mobile app, though, is as a platform for engaging both attendees and exhibitors, and for generating relevant statistics. The insights mobile apps unlock, and the capacity for those insights to impact big spending decisions, are some of the reasons investment activity in this subset of event tech is growing.

Organizers have shown that they will respond to cost and efficiency savings and, increasingly, to new revenue opportunities, which has helped spur the adoption of some event tech. As the industry changes, various traditional revenue streams will diminish and die, and fresh ones will spring up in their place. Every event organizer needs to be aware of opportunities to generate incremental revenue. Tools that allow them to do that will be very welcome, which means it's important that innovators know what to build.

Every constituency within the industry wants to understand and measure the metrics that determine whether an event is successful. They seek concrete tools to calculate ROI and engagement. Many don't realize how plausible these goals really are, and those who do are already excited.

We are excited as well. The face-to-face industry has remained remarkably the same for centuries. Over the past decade, with the advent of Twitter, Facebook, and smartphones, the influence of digital technology has become increasingly significant. Digital has begun to develop a presence at face-to-face events. Hopefully, the next phase will be the Cambrian explosion of digital tools for events.

For those of us who love both events and technology, it is thrilling to imagine how event tech will continue to evolve over the next few decades.

CHAPTER ONE

THE FEAR IN THE AIR

———

Never in human history has it been easier to connect with other people. We have an incredible range of communication tools and technologies at our fingertips, and most of us are glued to our smartphones for many of our waking hours.

Even as the number of ways we can connect is increasing, we've never been more isolated from one another. Until very recently, human beings lived in constant proximity. Now, our screens divide us as much as they bring us together. Constantly e-mailing, texting, and tweeting are no substitute for personal connection, which is why the face-to-face industry remains vibrant and important, even as digital technology becomes ever more widespread.

It's difficult to accurately quantify the size of the events industry. Some people think of events as trade shows. Others consider sports or concerts to be in the same category. Whatever the case, according to Frost and Sullivan, global spending on events, including transportation, accommodation, and other support, currently tops $565 billion.[4] That equates to more than five million meetings and events, with in excess of 512 million attendees.

Meeting Planners International (MPI) represents approximately 18,500 members in seventy-one countries. Together, these members top $22 billion in global buying power, of which approximately $11.5 billion is concentrated in the hands of some 4,800 planner members (event organizers).

There are numerous other large, successful organizations in the field. The Global Association of the Exhibition Industry (UFI), for example, represents hundreds of international exhibition organizers, venue operators, and exhibition service providers. The International Association of Exhibitions and Events (IAEE) represents 1,300 event organizers in fifty countries.

The Society of Independent Show Organizers (SISO) and the Professional Convention Management Association

4   http://www.slideshare.net/FrostandSullivan/event-management-software-market

(PCMA) provide members with regular access to education, networking, and industry information, while the Center for Exhibition Industry Research (CEIR) regularly produces quality research focused on topics relevant to the industry.

Clearly, the events industry is still a hugely relevant part of doing business. People attending events are usually more open to opportunity than those embedded in the daily grind. They have invested time, money, and energy to be there, and they want to meet people. In contrast, think about how likely you are to respond to a cold call or e-mail during a normal working week. The chances are that you will ignore it. Rapid advances in digital technology will not eliminate this facet of face-to-face events; indeed, they have the potential to amplify it. In the words of the MPI:

> By enabling effective face-to-face interactions, the meeting and event industry has had a profound impact on driving change, innovation, and economic growth for generations. The introduction and development of digital and web-based technologies is enabling event organizers to engage audiences in more interactive and innovative ways that enhance the attendee experience, increase innovation, and increase the ROI of events. This is an exciting time to be part of this influential and dynamic industry.

The most important thing to remember, however, is that technology is just a tool. As long as it's aligned to strategic business objectives and the strategic reasons for conducting a meeting, it can be extremely useful. But the temptation is to do what's new just because it's new.

As Kai Hattendorf, managing director of UFI, explains, it's easy to be pessimistic when faced with confusing changes, but the events industry has already shown great resilience in the face of digital disruption:

> Over the past twenty years, every time a digital development has become mainstream, experts have predicted the demise of the face-to-face exhibition industry.

> But neither the Internet, nor Second Life, nor social media have killed or even weakened the exhibition market. Quite the contrary: the Internet and digital communication channels have allowed regional players to become global players.

> With digitization now tying processes together, the links between marketers and marketplaces will become even closer. Today, an advanced trade show is far more than merely the right mix of exhibitors coming together in a venue. It is a complex construct of on-site and online services, tailored to serve specific industries.

HOW DIGITAL COULD CHANGE THE GAME

Event protocol has improved hugely over the years, but even today, it remains very clunky and inefficient. In the vast majority of cases, attendees often have no idea who else is participating in their chosen events. They are also accustomed to spending considerable time waiting in line before they even reach the registration desk, at which point, they receive a printed event directory. This directory, which usually offers the first insights into the identities of other participants and informs networking plans, is often large, unwieldy, and produced solely for the benefit of the organizer.

The only way to confirm the identities of other participants at a given event is to look up their contact details and give them a call. Some events offer basic information about which companies are likely to attend, but it's rarely possible to determine exactly who will be representing them.

Analyzing who will be at the event and booking appointments to meet them can create a lot of tension. Calling somewhere between ten and fifty companies, simply to ascertain whether the people you want to meet are going to be at the event you are attending, is a big job. Lots of potential attendees ultimately decide not to attend because they can't find the right people or don't want to spend time researching them. The stress only increases upon arrival.

Most events provide large orientation packs. Some of this information is valuable, such as maps, timetables, and information about sessions and speakers. Inevitably, however, some is irrelevant. Probably, some of it is also incorrect, due to last-minute changes that came about too late to be incorporated. Almost always, attendees find themselves carrying around great piles of paper that have little or nothing to do with their objectives for the event.

At the event itself, networking is a hit-or-miss proposition. It's difficult for attendees to know who people are or how their activities connect. People suffer from missed connections, spending entire events in close proximity to people who would have been perfect clients, but never realizing it. This often means that opportunities to do business go unnoticed until too late.

Meetings that *do* take place are characterized by an exchange of business cards and handouts, usually bearing scrawled telephone numbers. Following up requires a good memory. With so many different names and faces to remember, it is easy to forget the details of a conversation. All of this is compounded by event websites that look as though they haven't been updated since 1999, making them difficult to navigate and filled with irrelevant information.

Here's how we envisage the above changing as a result of digital innovation. You will be able to register well in advance of events via your computer or smartphone, saving you a long and boring wait to collect a name badge and receive orientation materials. This will help you to make the best use of your time and networking opportunities, maximizing your ROI.

Digital technology will invite you to explore the profiles of other event attendees. You can know who will be there in advance, what they're interested in buying or selling, and even what times they will be available to meet. Apps will enable you to identify when people you want to speak to are nearby, making it vastly easier to meet those you are most interested in connecting with.

If you want to exchange information, you will no longer need to find a scrap of paper, locate a pen, and scribble down your name and number. Instead, you can use a mobile app to swap contact details quickly and easily. These details will probably include a photograph to jog your memory when you call your new connection.

Similarly, literature will be easily transferred in a digital format, giving you a library of information at your fingertips, instead of a cumbersome bag full of soon-to-be-outdated material. In addition, mobile technology will make navigating the show floor much easier than it used to be. You will even be able to program mobile apps to give you suggestions, based on your interests and needs, and to plot a path that takes you to the exhibits you want to visit.

Some of the above is already taking shape. Some of it may sound like science fiction. At the time of writing, all the individual applications exist, but the various technologies are not sufficiently well integrated to provide a coherent experience. The situation is much better than it used to be, but this is still only the tip of the iceberg.

Imagine a scenario in which you can be notified when people in your LinkedIn network register for an event and be offered the opportunity to schedule a meeting with them. Alternatively, let's say you refer several friends from a different company to the event. How will you know whether they registered unless you make a point of calling each one to find out? How much easier would it be to make a digital connection and let an app update you on their status? The data exists. The raw materials exist. They only need to be put together.

Technology is the key to improving the experiences of attendees, making it easier to navigate events efficiently and use them profitably. This trend will only continue as the platforms advance. In future, for example, we foresee VR and AR/MR developments that will change the way potential clients interact with products they're interested in.

It should be possible to collect information digitally, to connect with people on LinkedIn at the tap of a button, and to file new connections automatically in your customer relationship management (CRM) system. It should also be possible to find the people you want to meet. Beacons is a technology that locates people in your vicinity, making it easier to know when those you're interested in talking to are close by. It is already being rolled out, and some events are proud to proclaim that more than 50 percent of their attendees have downloaded the Beacons mobile app.

Events offer a unique opportunity to meet people with a similar, complementary intent. Everyone who participates in an event has an intention for being there, even if they don't truly understand it. Retail stores already understand this and collect data accordingly. They arrange displays in ways that have been shown to attract attention. They alter the layout of their stores to maximize purchases.

In the events world, this kind of data is only just beginning to be widely available. Many people still think of event organization as a simple matter of hiring a space in which people can set up booths. Increasingly, however, events are becoming a complex data problem, based on discovering intent and understanding how to satisfy it.

Why, then, is digital innovation not embraced more warmly within the industry? Why, in fact, does it often seem that key players in the face-to-face events industry fear the advent of digital, as opposed to welcoming it?

A VOLATILE INDUSTRY, ALREADY IN FLUX

We concluded the previous section by asking why the dominant attitude toward tech from incumbent event organizers seems hesitant. The answer, as we touched on in the introduction to this book, is that it's difficult to predict the direction of future change, and people are nervous that their livelihoods will be negatively impacted. It's too early to tell who will win and who will lose as digital technology becomes ever more widespread in the events arena. The volatile nature of the events industry compounds this unpredictability.

Consider the fate of Comdex, once the largest technology show in the world. The main event took place annually, in Las Vegas, with other Comdex-branded shows also scheduled around the world. Much like the Consumer Electronics Show (CES) in the present day, Comdex was extremely successful and profitable, a Goliath among trade events. So much so that, in 2001, Comdex's founder, Sheldon Adelson, sold the show to Softbank, a large Japanese financial and technology group, for $800 million.[5] Within three years, however, Comdex was essentially dead.

From an asset perspective, trade shows are a rare breed. When run well, they can be highly profitable and enduring. They are also highly volatile. Purchasers of trade shows are paying for access to brands and databases, along with the services of the people who execute the events. There is a lot of money riding on the goodwill of those stakeholders. The value of trade shows lies in the fact that people want to attend them and, despite appearances, truly understanding why people attend and whether they will continue to do so in the future is arguably more art than science. As Comdex illustrates, it doesn't take much for a giant to fall. Worse, when that fall happens, it's no mere decline. It's a total collapse.

The story of Comdex is a cautionary tale for everyone in the face-to-face environment. It reminds us how quickly fortunes can change, and simultaneously highlights and helps to explain the cautious nature of incumbents within the events industry.

---

5   http://articles.latimes.com/1995-02-14/business/fi-31862_1_u-s-trade-shows

As described above, technology is undoubtedly impacting various aspects of the face-to-face events industry. What we need to know is how significant those changes will ultimately prove. Will technology radically redefine the structure of events? Airbnb, for example, is not killing the hotel business. Instead, it is creating an entirely new category of hospitality experience. It's possible that as digital technology develops, we will witness the development of entirely new categories of events.

In the Internet era, technology has made it incalculably easier to access information. In the mobile era, the impact of technology has become more three-dimensional. It lives with us in a way that would have been hard to predict even a decade ago and influences every aspect of our lives. The mobile era has forced us to think of the Internet and digital technology in a whole new way, one that encompasses not just information and connections between people, but also time and space.

Big data is a technology buzzword at the moment, as is the Internet of Things (IoT). We have the capacity to collect data that has never been available before, and that data leads to previously unimaginable possibilities. Combine big data and IoT and, on the consumer front, it's realistic to surmise that, within the next five years, it will be possible for your fridge to communicate with your local grocery store, placing orders automatically when you run out of things that you buy regularly, and having a drone drop it on your doorstep. Within the next decade, this will also include a robotic home assistant that puts the items in your fridge.

Events, in our clearly biased point of view, represent a massive and hugely underestimated opportunity because they incorporate all these technological applications and more. Attendees want to access relevant information, facilitate relationships, *and* find ways of using their time and navigating their environment more effectively. The potential applications of technology in the events industry are enormous, but relatively few people are concentrating their attention there. Ironically, advances in technology could themselves give rise to new shows, where consumers and companies will meet in person to understand advancements in tech: eventception.

Approximately ten years ago, the concept of virtual trade shows became briefly popular. Why spend time and money to attend events in person when you can experience many of the same things from your machine? That was the theory, at least. The reality didn't match the hype, however. The technology was buggy and inefficient, and the experience of sitting at a computer was boring and unsatisfying in comparison with the experience of meeting people face-to-face.

It's possible that this idea is due for a comeback. Technology has improved significantly in the intervening decade, increasing the potential to create a truly immersive environment. Younger generations are already growing up as digital natives, familiar with VR and AR/MR. Perhaps within the next twenty years, they will crack the code and develop technologies that make digital trade shows a genuinely rewarding experience. Alternatively, perhaps they will fulfill the cynical expectations of the older generation by proving that they really do prefer interacting with one another through a device rather than in person.

Rather than one big disruption, such as Uber, we think it's more likely that the face-to-face industry will experience many small disruptions. While we don't believe that there's an Uber waiting in the wings, ready to unveil a completely new paradigm of events, that's no reason for event organizers to be complacent. If you're in the industry, now is a good time to start analyzing research about emerging technological experiments. Take note of what is on the horizon and be willing to embrace new marketing tools, technologies, and trends. It's important to ride the wave of change as it crests, not to miss it and be left gasping for breath as it breaks.

Consumer expectations are changing, and this is perhaps both the greatest unknown and the most critical factor in the development of event tech. In the past, event organizers had the relatively simple, pragmatic role of creating itineraries based on a set roster of buyers and sellers, on a specific date, at a specific venue.

While all those aspects of event creation are still valid today, event organizers are increasingly aware of the need to understand deeper layers of interaction and matchmaking, both in person and online. Communities extend beyond the face-to-face elements of events, and it's becoming imperative for event organizers to understand how their clients interact during the rest of the year.

This last point is one we can't emphasize strongly enough. Events used to be the epicenter of industry activity, and, while they still are in many industries, they no longer get to dictate the other 363 days of the year the way they once did. Organizers must become much more responsive to those changes, a role very unfamiliar to many of them. Modern event organizers still need to bring together the right buyers and sellers, book the best speakers, and match content and audience. The big difference is that that's no longer sufficient.

Event organizers must become much more than simply planners or relationship brokers. Modern airlines must still focus on performing their key task of transporting people from one place to another, but now they are also in the relationship business. They are judged and compared on their customer service. Something similar is true of event organizers, who must understand people in a way they have never needed to before.

In the words of Donald Pazour, president and CEO of Access Intelligence: "At the heart of the event industry is the goal of producing worthwhile face-to-face three-dimensional experiences for buyers and sellers." This, he says, can only be done in a sustainable way if there is "a sense of community among buyers and buyers, buyers and sellers, and sellers and sellers."

The creation of a good event is becoming a social science with a digital component. As we like to say, it's a mixture of digital strategy and physical serendipity. Event organizers need to understand the motivations and behavior of their audiences, including their online activities. A lot of people are very nervous about this shift. They like the roles they are accustomed to playing, and they're uncomfortable altering them. Unfortunately, they may not have a choice in the matter.

To this point, a lot of technological advances in the events industry have been consumer driven. So many people use mobile phones, and prefer not to waste paper, that event organizers are under pressure to offer a mobile-compatible option for accessing content. They still make more money from printed materials, but the expectations of attendees have become so powerful that they can no longer be ignored.

Similarly, people tweet, so virtually every brand uses a hashtag for promotional purposes. Brands without hashtags are behind the curve. What's still missing is a concerted, industry-wide effort to adopt technology *proactively*, as opposed to reactively.

A BETTER RESPONSE THAN FEAR

Fear may seem a natural response to the menu of changes likely to affect the events industry in the coming years. We question, however, whether it's the *right* response. Robert Augustus Masters says that "fear is excitement in drag."

In other words, it's possible to reframe the fear of change by perceiving that change as an opportunity to grow and learn, and by focusing on how exciting it can be to do new things and open up new possibilities. It's easy to be scared, but no one ever transformed a business through living in fear. Excitement, intrigue, and curiosity are far more effective drivers of positive action.

Let's revisit the examples of Airbnb and Uber. Some people in the hospitality and travel industries greeted their emergence by becoming paralyzed, unable to accept the rapid change in the game and unwilling to respond proactively. Others approached Airbnb and Uber with curiosity, asking how they could learn from the principles those companies were using to succeed and adapting their own activities accordingly.

Accor Hotels, for example, responded to the rise of Airbnb by acquiring Onefinestay, a high-end version of Airbnb that includes more hotel services, for at least $170 million, and committing to at least $70 million of further investment over the coming years.[6]

In the events industry, the smartest people are already preparing for change. They understand that they need to be brave and to experiment. They recognize the value of investing time, money, and resources in understanding the potential of digital technology. They are willing to fail fast and learn from their mistakes in order to be ready to embrace change as it hits.

Good entrepreneurs are always aware of the ways their industry is evolving and the challenges that evolution will bring. They stay abreast of the activities of their

6   https://techcrunch.com/2016/04/04/accorhotels-acquires-onefinestay-for-170-million/

competitors and accept that, if they fail to identify the direction in which the industry is moving, they will be left behind. Spotting trends is a difficult and unpredictable activity, but it can be extremely productive. The people who take a long view can gain a crucial edge, seeing shifts earlier and capitalizing on them swiftly.

One of our aims is to encourage members of the events industry to take a positive view of the opportunities promised by digital technology. By responding with curiosity and courage, we can lift the entire industry.

Typically, as you might expect in a field with an 850-year history, the events industry has been conservative and resistant to change. We are starting to hear, however, from people who already feel that if they continue on their current path, they will soon be out of business. These people recognize the need to alter their mindset and their company culture. They realize that an open mind is essential to understand the influence of digital technology on their livelihoods.

The face-to-face industry is encountering new realities. The communities of people who organize and attend events interact regularly and communicate in new, powerful ways. It's easier than ever to share information and learn from one another. Unless we are willing to embrace new paradigms and new technologies, many events will suffer, becoming less and less relevant to their respective industries and communities.

The good news is that there's a better response than fear. Get curious about the changes already having an impact on the industry and the trends that indicate what may be around the corner. Those who can predict the future successfully will own it. In the next chapter, we'll examine the changes being wrought by digital technology in greater depth, exploring individual case studies and industry-wide trends to paint a picture of the entire landscape. How is technology already making an impact in the events sphere? Which aspects of events are most affected? Just as importantly, where are the glaring holes in the landscape and the areas of greatest need?

CHAPTER TWO

TECTONIC FORCES AT PLAY

———

After remaining broadly the same for nearly a thousand years, why is the face-to-face events industry changing *now*? What are the forces catalyzing change in an industry that has been one of the most stable and consistent in human history?

Just as importantly, *what* are the changes that are already beginning to emerge, and what impact are they having on the industry? In the previous chapter, we discussed change in broad terms, linking the rise of digital technology with the potential for disruption, or positive change, in the face-to-face industry. In this chapter, we'll explore some technological innovations in more depth, detailing their value and exploring the questions about digital integration that remain unanswered.

As described in chapter one, technology has traditionally been a top-down phenomenon. Network television is broadcast from a central studio to an audience of people who don't have the option of creating their own shows. YouTube, by contrast, offers anyone with a smartphone the opportunity to produce videos. In 2017, everyone is a technologist. Tech is no longer tech; tech is everything. Alternatively, as Marc Andreessen phrased it, "Software is eating the world." He said this more than five years ago, and today, it is more relevant than ever.

This move toward accessible technology is also changing people's expectations. Increasingly, technology is integrated seamlessly into almost every aspect of our daily lives. If it's possible to plan journeys, book hotels, and surf the Internet on our mobile phones, the expectation that it will soon become possible to simplify and streamline the experience of attending events looks like an eminently reasonable one.

Airbnb is an example of a technological innovation that connects people with one another and involves everyone with a stake in the process. Instead of operating from the top down, it collects data from the bottom up, using that data to present potential clients with accommodation options. Uber and Lyft connect people who want to go somewhere with drivers willing to take them.

Consider a music festival such as South by Southwest (SXSW). Previously, people relied on centrally organized taxis to provide them with transport to their hotels. Now, they can book an Uber or Lyft driver to take them to their Airbnb residence. Uber has recently started operating in Nevada, with a mission to shift the experience of attendees of the Consumer Electronics Show (CES) in Las Vegas by dramatically reducing waiting time for taxis.

Airbnb, too, sees an opportunity. Hundreds of rooms in the local area will be available for visitors to Las Vegas to rent, probably at rates lower than those offered by comparable hotels, while CES is taking place. The underlying needs remain the same. People need places to stay and transport. The ways those needs are being met, however, are on the move.

CONSUMER POWER AND TECHNOLOGICAL INNOVATION

In a sense, this is an uprising of consumer power. Disruptions such as those instigated by Uber and Airbnb are not altering the landscapes of entire industries by creating better tech. They are doing it by using tech to craft entirely new experiences and reshape the expectations of users. Often, incumbents are shocked by the speed of change and forced into a reactive stance as they see their business models threatened by newcomers. They tend to focus on protecting their businesses instead of serving their customers.

In comparison with the face-to-face industry, cars and telephones are relatively recent innovations. They have histories of around 100 years, as opposed to the 850-year pedigree of face-to-face events. That history may have an impact on how technological developments are viewed within the events industry. There is, perhaps, less of a sense of urgency than in other fields. The events ecosystem has survived much greater changes than the creation of a new app. Nonetheless, events certainly aren't immune to the impact of innovation, or the damage that can be done from relying on a reactive approach to the inescapable changes that technology brings.

One of the key messages of this book is that a reactive approach to technological change will not be sufficient to propel the events industry forward. Now is the time to embrace new opportunities, new technologies, and the new models they portend. Investing in technology and talent now can improve the industry's capacity to respond effectively to change and even to *lead* those changes, as opposed to being forced into reacting to technological innovations as they emerge.

This is why it is so important to invest capital in technological innovation *now*, while the field is still open. Change will be driven by those who are prepared to see what's coming and shape the future, and the events industry has much room for improvement in this field. The incentive structures that should be in place to attract and reward top talent are not there, making the industry relatively unattractive as a place to innovate. Changes will come, but if we don't drive those changes from within the industry, they will be driven from outside, in potentially disruptive ways.

Ultimately, we'd like to see the events industry play host to technology incubators and benefit from ring-fenced event technology funding. As an industry, it's important that we chart our own future. This will provide us with freedom to innovate and to make the events space a much more welcoming place for the next generation of talent.

Capitalization delivers the freedom to innovate. Money 2020 is an annual gathering for companies at the intersection of financial services, payments, and e-commerce. The show enjoyed a meteoric rise and was sold for a high figure. The founders then raised $2.5 million to launch a new show. This level of capitalization is highly unusual for an event launch and allows the organizing team to invest in whatever methods they see fit, without the constraints of a more traditional holding company.

Most shows, however, do not have the deep pockets of Money 2020. Their organizers are focused on the balance sheet, and investing significant sums in unproven technology looks like a risky move. Research and development is a precarious endeavor. Some products inevitably fail. For the industry as a whole, however, this phase is not optional. The face-to-face environment needs an infusion of money and talent to keep up with the rapid changes digital technologies are bringing to the arena.

For big international organizers, this is a fine line. They are already investing marginal quantities of cash and resources in digital and tech innovations, aware that change is on the way. If they move too aggressively, however, they risk exerting such a powerful influence that their core businesses will be impacted. Timing is everything.

Let's clarify by exploring some of the major areas of change and showing how innovative software is already permeating the events ecosystem.

Almost every visitor or exhibitor at a given show uses a mobile phone. In fact, scratch that. If visitors don't have their mobile phones with them at all times, they are missing huge opportunities. According to *Perkins Internet Report*, mobile usage is now greater than more traditional web access.[7] If you're looking to promote an event, mobile must be a huge part of your marketing plan.

It's an amazing tool. One of your authors (Marco) is on the board of DoubleDutch, a leading company in the mobile category. DoubleDutch is a San Francisco-based company focused on creating a digital engagement marketing platform to help event organizers and their customers engage with mobile and digital solutions like never before.

In previous years, attendees at trade shows received directories, which were usually big books containing information about exhibitors, visitors, and conferences. Already, many events are moving toward mobile apps that collate all that information, making it easy for participants to interact with the app. They can identify the exhibits they want to visit, the conferences they want to attend, and the people they want to connect with.

7   http://www.kpcb.com/blog/2016-internet-trends-report

This mobile approach is giving visitors and exhibitors an entirely new experience of events. Mobile technology is assisting them in attracting the people they are most interested in and connecting with their most important contacts. Once people have actually *met*, mobile technology gives them access to content and information that wasn't available previously.

Mobile tech is infiltrating every aspect of our lives. Why wouldn't it influence the way we participate in events? Most importantly, it has become such an integral part of daily life that its usage is no longer a bonus: it's an expectation. Mobile tech is an essential part of human interaction in the twenty-first century. The face-to-face events world must respond to this reality if those of us who are part of it are to shape our own futures, as opposed to seeing them shaped for us.

TECHNOLOGY SIMPLIFIES REGISTRATION AND TICKETING

Disney has created the "MagicBand," a premium pass offered to guests at Disney resorts. Those who stay in Disney-branded hotels or who subscribe to the company's membership offering receive MagicBands free of additional charge. Others have the opportunity to purchase them. These bands make navigating Disney properties simpler and easier. They can be used to unlock hotel rooms, charge food and merchandise, enter theme and water parks, and check in at specific entrances to attractions, allowing wearers to avoid lines.

The company has invested more than a billion dollars in the creation of MagicBands.[8]

For those who love Disney and want their holiday experiences to be special, they represent a chance to smooth out the wrinkles that sometimes create stress and frustration during vacations.

What impact could this kind of innovation have on the face-to-face industry? In theory, it should be entirely possible to run event registration on a model similar to the one used in the creation of the MagicBand. Why shouldn't event attendees receive a wristband or pass that they can use to gain access to an event, instead of standing in line waiting to register?

On the subject of registration, event technology related to ticketing received 355 investments in the year leading up to March 2016, totaling $1.25 billion, according to the Tracxn event management report. The best-funded company was Eventbrite, which received $200 million

8   https://www.wired.com/2015/03/disney-magicband/

from investors, including highly respected firms such as Sequoia Capital.

Historically, event owners and operators have built websites to launch new events and sell tickets. Building a website is often a slow and arduous process, and the results are mixed. Sometimes sites come out looking quite ugly. Eventbrite has changed all this.

The Eventbrite website allows users to create customized event pages and manage registration online. Instead of passing through a cumbersome, clunky, and visually unappealing process, prospective attendees can visit attractive, easy-to-use sites that guide them toward registration in a pleasant and frictionless fashion.

For modern tech users, a clean, intuitive experience is vital. Prettiness is no longer an optional extra; it's an indispensable design element. Sites need to look good and work well, otherwise they will contribute to attrition. Unless your web checkout process is slick and seamless, people will lose interest.

For event organizers, Eventbrite eliminates the need for a dedicated tech team. They no longer need to know how to build web pages or to employ someone who does. Instead, they have a tool that makes it easy to put together web pages that are better than the ones used by most enterprises. The service has spawned a new breed of event organizer, generated a lot of competition, and enabled almost anyone to produce quick, professional event websites.

WEBSITE OPTIMIZATION INCREASES SALES

Another company already enjoying success in the event-tech space is Optimizely. Optimizely has reinvented the concept of A/B testing, which is a method of comparing two different versions of an app or web page to determine which one performs better. Clearly, the results of well-designed A/B tests are very valuable. They give businesses an unbiased window into the minds of their customers, allowing them to pick the most attractive versions of their pages and make more sales.

Prior to the creation of Optimizely, this was a difficult process to manage. Most individuals didn't have the resources to tackle it effectively, while employees of larger companies generally lacked the freedom to experiment with different variables. They needed central approval, which was usually time-consuming to attain.

Optimizely makes it easy for marketers to perform A/B tests on their own, with no special expertise. Like

Eventbrite, it has unleashed an entirely new group of people into the industry, placing pressure on marketplace incumbents to perform.

Some of the tools now available to anyone are not merely as good as those used by most professional event management firms; they are better. Until recently, companies believed that they held an unassailable advantage due to their far greater resources. Now, their insider status is beginning to actively hinder their progress, because it makes them slower to see and utilize changes that outsiders are quick to spot and leverage.

DATA ANALYTICS AND REPORTING PRESENT NEW INSIGHTS

Events are rich sources of data with the potential to provide deep and powerful insights. Up to the present day, event organizers have largely been inefficient in the way they have captured and used data, but new tools are opening up fresh potential. Organizers, exhibitors, and sponsors can all capture data in ways that have never previously been available.

Feathr is one of the companies your authors have invested in. It's a specialized marketing tool that collects data from exhibitors and visitors in ways that would have been impossible five years ago. Unlike most marketing tools, it's aimed specifically at the events industry, allowing users to understand, grow, and engage with their audiences.

Aleksander Levental, one of the founders of Feathr, explains why he sees events as such uniquely fertile ground:

> The events industry is not standing at a precipice of instantaneous and unilateral change. Rather, we're looking ahead to a rolling landscape of hills and valleys that complicate strategy and obscure the destination. Publishers have experienced a similar set of circumstances and challenges over the last twenty years. The combination of evolving technology, culture, and industry has required publishers to continuously reevaluate both their product and business model, and events are about to be stressed in exactly the same ways.

> As face-to-face experiences become more precious in life, people will seek out live experiences with greater commitment, while being more discriminating about how and where they spend their time. Events have the unique opportunity to combine digital and live experiences for consumers and business more richly than any other channel. Delivering on that opportunity, however, will require a commitment to years of innovation, patience, and self-evaluation.

There have been efforts to collect and collate data relating to events for some time, but until recently, that data hasn't been mined effectively for valuable insights. It hasn't been monetized or used to create new offerings based on customer behavior and preferences. At the time of writing, that's changing rapidly. Event organizers are waking up to the understanding that their databases are potential goldmines and are seeking out the tools they need to mine this gold.

The goal of event technology tools is to allow everyone involved in events to benefit: organizers, exhibitors, and attendees. High-quality data should lead everyone toward more efficient usage of time and money. Eventbrite handles the creation of websites and the simplification of registration. That's a great first step. The next logical step is data capture.

How do you know whether people are interacting with your sites or apps, and whether they're doing what you want them to do? Until recently, this question hasn't been a priority for most people in the face-to-face industry. Witnessing the activities of retail stores, such as heat mapping and sentiment analysis, has inspired leaders in the events space to recognize the potential of data.

Imagine how useful it would be to understand the foot traffic patterns of people walking around exhibition halls.

What could that tell us? Arguably, it could present insights into the ideal locations of premium booths, along with a salable rationale for increased costs. It's relatively easy for event organizers to sell the idea of variable prices if they can demonstrate that the more expensive booths receive significantly more traffic. This technology already exists and is increasing exponentially in sophistication and accuracy. Now, we need only translate it into a form that is accessible to, and usable by, event organizers.

Another angle is that understanding foot traffic patterns could make it easier to influence traffic. Recognizing what attracts people to specific locations opens up the possibility of improving the desirability of specific sites. At present, it's not easy to know how people respond to the content they absorb in sessions. Paper surveys are of questionable reliability. Technology has the potential to provide far more accurate feedback and can be used to log the movements and pulses of attendees, providing valuable information about their engagement levels.

The events industry needs to get better at using data, making the analytics more accessible and revealing. Freeman is a company focused on making data *personal*. What does this mean? It's about making sure that the data being collected has a practical application that improves the lives of those who use it. Bob Priest-Heck, president of Freeman, says, "People will be the next killer app," and asks, "Does the technology narrow the gap between people, or does it create a barrier? Change is not about bombarding people with gadgets and apps. It's about making the experience richer, the wasted time shorter, and the connections as broad or as deep as people want them to be." For example, sales representatives might collect data that tells them what their audience is interested in. That data may reveal previously overlooked potential buyers for a new product.

Google Analytics has become a standard tool for modern online businesses. Thanks to mobile phones, the scope for collecting data continues to increase. In the events field in particular, this is an incredibly exciting time, in an area ripe for innovation. This is precisely why an investment fund would be such a valuable addition to the industry. If it were possible to collaborate in the creation of an "adventure fund," which provided smart people with the funds they needed to solve problems, that fund could finance the industry's future competitiveness.

It's essential that as event tech evolves, we become more tightly focused on measuring results. We must not lose sight of the criteria by which stakeholders judge us. The industry needs recognizable criteria for determining success and return on investment (ROI).

Richard Maranville of Freeman sees it this way: "If we can figure out how to quantify what most everyone believes is a great investment, that could help increase the quality and number of events. The one thing we should be able to get from going digital is a better sense of ROI at every level." Quantifying the value of investments is essential to fueling the development of further solutions and assessing which innovations are working effectively. Online retailers such as Amazon and Netflix are already analyzing data in great depth and using what they learn to craft compelling offerings. There's no reason why the events industry can't follow suit.

MARKETING AND ADVERTISING TECHNOLOGY ARE REPLACING OUTDATED METHODS

Web developers are easy to find. Driving more traffic, especially the right traffic, to your site is more complex. What are the best ways to motivate people to buy tickets for an event and, even better, to become active advocates? The solutions lie in marketing and advertising technology.

At the time of writing, the events industry suffers from a dearth of these, despite the fact that the sector contends with very similar challenges when compared to other large industries. Event organizers need website traffic and methods of analyzing visitor numbers and behavior.

They need to send e-mail and monitor open rates, clicks, and conversions.

The industry is not likely to be disrupted by external marketing and ad-tech solutions. Those solutions already exist. Nonetheless, event organizers are falling behind in their ability to maximize ticket sales and returns for sponsors, simply because they don't have access to best-of-breed digital tools.

Marketing and ad tech represent great opportunities for event organizers to improve efficiency. Fifteen years ago, events were promoted primarily through marketing by mail. Now, that approach looks archaic. Marketing tech has taken over. In other industries, this change has already had a huge impact. The face-to-face industry, however, has been slow to embrace it. Feathr is not reinventing the wheel. The company is simply adjusting existing tools in a way that makes them easy to use and affordable from the perspectives of event organizers, exhibitors, sponsors, and visitors.

There are numerous other players in this field, including InGo, SplashThat, and SpinGo. They are gradually gaining traction, especially when they create attractive user experiences that make it easy for those in the face-to-face field to use them. Despite the relatively low levels of adoption, there are already many tools available in the events space. There are so many, in fact—more than 1,600, according to the latest Tracxn report, released in January 2017—that space prohibits discussing them all in this book.

Nonetheless, we'll discuss one instructive example: landing pages. Almost every marketer operating online uses landing pages. They are an essential tool for testing and selling products and ideas. There are numerous tools that enable marketers to build and test landing pages, but those tools are not usually optimized for the needs of event organizers and promoters.

Events often connect thousands of sponsors, exhibitors, and visitors. The ideal scenario for event organizers is to see their sponsors and exhibitors e-mailing clients to encourage them to attend events. This is best achieved by creating custom landing pages, which offer a more personal experience than simply referring people to generic event sites.

Cobranded pages are more appealing to sponsors and exhibitors than pages that promote only those events with which they are partnering. Sponsors and exhibitors need to feel that shows belong to them, too, and putting their names on only the main show pages of websites doesn't accomplish this objective.

This is why Feathr, for example, allows sponsors and exhibitors to promote custom, sponsor-branded pages. For sponsors and exhibitors, this move makes outreach feel more personal. They are also more likely to benefit directly from the goodwill generated by such outreach. In the context of their own promotional efforts, and in the eyes of their clients, sponsors and exhibitors get to feel unique and differentiated. The best shows become the best because those in attendance want to share their experiences. The onus is on organizers, both to actively encourage their supporters to share their attendance and to make it easier and more attractive for them to do so.

ONLINE EDUCATION TECHNOLOGY: NEW PRODUCTS FROM UNDERUSED INFORMATION

It's not uncommon for organizations to invest millions of dollars in conferences, trade shows, festivals, sports or music events lasting no more than a few days. When those events are over, the content is no longer accessible. The money invested in creating it and putting the event together generates no further returns.

Some companies are working to solve the problem of online education as a facet of event creation. FORA.tv, for example, offers video production and online distribution based on events. Imagine an event where four thousand people are watching a conference or listening to a keynote speech. It's likely many people in the room will be distracted by phones, tablets, or computers and are therefore paying little attention to the speaker. This is a huge problem, but it's also a huge opportunity. Freeman invites users to interact with conferences from their devices, restoring their engagement levels.

Online video is an exceptionally powerful medium, but purveyors of online video require great content to be successful. The face-to-face industry naturally creates a lot of exceptional content, providing an opportunity both to leverage value and to improve the digital experience of millions of event attendees. It's imperative that the events industry tap into this resource and find better and more creative ways to share content online, extending the value cycle of events.

In 2015, Snapchat hosted more than forty million user-generated videos taken at Coachella. Periscope and Meerkat are also useful tools. The potential of online video to broaden the scope of face-to-face events, involving both attendees and those who cannot attend in person, is enormous. Harnessing this potential should be a priority for the industry.

It's likely that in the coming years, we will see many more smart entrepreneurs creating tools that can enhance audience engagement and be used to build online networks that will ultimately translate into live event communities.

Shows may take place over the course of a few days, but their influence and footprints extend much further. Modern event organizers need to find ways to generate engagement far beyond the narrow window of time occupied by the actual face-to-face experience. This is what we call the "365" model of events.

Attendees of specific events become part of the communities that surround those events. Those communities remain active online throughout the year, pursuing shared objectives. For some communities, the goals may be based on education. Other communities may support trade or, in the case of business-to-consumer shows such as Comic Con, simply bring people together to swap stories and have fun.

Some companies already offer software that enables exhibitors, visitors, and sponsors to interact. They can upload products and services to a common platform, creating a foundation for ongoing communication. When these platforms are effective, they keep communities alive all year long, increasing both the number of participants and their levels of interaction.

Shows have long been places where transactions occur and buyers and sellers meet. Buying cycles, however, are now expanding. Where buying was once concentrated around shows, it is now spread throughout the year. The value propositions of event organizers have always been based on the capacity to bring people together and facilitate transactions. If they lose that privileged position, the industry as a whole will suffer.

This is why a 365 approach to client interaction is required. As yet, this trend is still developing, so it's unclear exactly how it will unfold. Which elements will emerge as the most valuable? Knowledge sharing? Private social networks? Facilitating transactions? Perhaps networks built within networks, such as LinkedIn groups set up for specific purposes, will prove most valuable. Maybe smart event managers will find ways of bringing clients together online, hosting events that, in effect, run constantly. If they succeed, the entire industry will be revolutionized. The added value for organizers and exhibitors will be enormous.

It's too soon to state unequivocally what direction the movement toward a 365 approach will take. What is clear, however, is that this shift toward building communities that operate throughout the year is a fascinating and compelling phenomenon, and that it will change the way events are perceived. Shows are no longer annual propositions. They are evolving into launch pads for wider communities.

So far, the most successful versions of 365 are based around knowledge sharing. Some are private, while others are built on the platforms provided by existing social networks, such as Facebook and LinkedIn. Some facilitate smaller face-to-face meetings during the course of the year.

In the television industry, there are four or five global events each year. At other times, however, TV producers, channels, and stations struggle to create dynamic trade interactions. Rights Trade is a European company set up specifically to meet this challenge. Rights are traded through the organization's website throughout the year, but it has no intention of replacing the face-to-face element of the industry. Trade shows are critical in sustaining the ecosystem they're part of.

Could players in the 365 sphere step in and do to the face-to-face landscape what Airbnb has done to the hospitality space? It's easy to assume that because online solutions are so powerful and easy to use, they will simply usurp face-to-face events entirely. At least in the short term, however, that solution is not so easy to implement. Companies such as Balluun.com are not in direct competition with trade shows. Instead, they operate as business-to-business marketplaces, complementing the live-event experience. Nonetheless, companies may look at the online world and decide that, instead of investing a couple of millions of dollars per year on trade shows, they can halve their investment and procure online solutions that are easy to measure and highly cost-effective.

MATCHMAKING: THE SEARCH FOR THE TINDER OF EVENTS

Digital technology makes it extremely easy to connect, but it also makes it very easy to *dis*connect. Unfriending someone on Facebook or unfollowing them on Twitter are the work of a moment. This makes it much harder to develop trust in online relationships than in face-to-face ones. It also creates an echo chamber in which online filters direct us toward people likely to agree with us and away from people likely to disagree, arguably reducing the ability to tolerate conflict and perspectives different from our own.

Dating apps and websites, such as Tinder and Match.com, have succeeded in bridging the gap between online and face-to-face connection, creating fortunes in the process. The old-school model of dating, based on face-to-face connections with people in the same community, is dying. Technology makes it so much easier to meet people than it used to be, especially in cities, that slow, painstaking investment in a single person looks anachronistic.

Some tech innovators are aiming to do the same thing in the events industry, using artificial intelligence (AI) and sophisticated algorithms in an effort to match buyers and sellers at events. This task is more difficult than it appears, but there are some very dedicated people working hard to crack it.

The amount of information required to match buyers and sellers effectively, coupled with the complexities of the industry and the difficulties of matching people when they are in the same vicinity, has so far prevented anyone from designing an app that really works. There are a lot more variables involved in putting buyers in front of sellers than there are in connecting two people who are interested in dating.

As with every other problem that is also an opportunity, we know it will be solved. We just don't know when. The online dating industry is huge and exceptionally profitable. It's also very effective. Event organizers have been wondering for a while how they can learn from and adapt a dating model to a business context.

At the time of writing, there are approximately different start-ups tackling the problem, and your authors are investors in one of them—Grip. Based in London, Grip is supported by some exceptional European tech entrepreneurs.

While there are numerous highly intelligent entrepreneurs seeking to tackle this problem, no definitive solution has yet been reached. The potential, however, is huge. Trade shows and conferences represent an exceptional opportunity to use technology for matchmaking, because both buyer and seller are already in the right mindset to generate transactions when attending trade shows. The challenge is the large amount of information required to identify the right buyers and sellers and to connect them with one another. As yet, it's quite difficult to collect all that information, and it tends to arrive in a fragmented form.

Putting all the pieces together is a complicated conundrum, but the code will undoubtedly be cracked. All the necessary technology already exists. It's simply a matter of making it all work together in a way that is smooth and attractive from a user perspective. A combination of websites, registration technology, AI, and mobile apps holds the key.

Matchmaking is more than simply tagging or making referrals. It's an integrated process of identifying compatible requests made by buyers and sellers and facilitating connections that will lead to transactions. The industry as a whole must do a better job of matchmaking. As described in the introduction of this book, one of the primary functions of event organizers is to act as relationship brokers, bringing people together who might otherwise never have met and done business. As such, mastering online matchmaking represents a key area of expansion for the face-to-face ecosystem.

Some event organizers and marketers may not particularly *want* to address the problems of matchmaking, but it's a necessity driven by shifting consumer expectations. Just as e-commerce customers are coming to expect free shipping with their purchases, attendees of face-to-face events increasingly expect technological integration. They are customers of several businesses and will undoubtedly favor those companies that resolve the challenges of matchmaking most quickly.

Companies that offer exclusive products and services are somewhat protected by the nature of their businesses, but customers are becoming less and less tolerant of poor service. It's always possible to imitate a product.

Another reason to tackle the question of matchmaking is that people are increasingly busy. In past decades, event attendees may have been willing to peruse every exhibit in search of what they needed. Today, they are concerned with maximizing ROI. They want to know who they should meet and receive assistance in facilitating that connection.

Many people come to shows precisely because they know that specific buyers or sellers will also attend, so it's natural that they expect contacting those people to be as easy as possible. One of the most common requests we field at events comes from people who want to see the attendee list. Understandably, they are annoyed when events don't provide such a list because they don't have an easy way to contact other participants and arrange meetings.

In the past, event attendees were used to simply hunting for the people they wanted to connect with. Now, they see the ability to connect quickly with the people they are interested in as a necessity. Events that don't meet that expectation can anticipate falling ticket sales.

There is another side to this situation. It's not wise to give out e-mail addresses in an attendee list. Were event organizers to start doing this, a certain subset of buyers would be overwhelmed with requests to connect, to the extent that they might be afraid to walk the hall and unwilling to rebook. It's important to give people a route to connect but not make that route so easy that it results in some participants feeling harassed.

There's a considerable difference between contacting someone on LinkedIn and forging a genuine business partnership. In comparison with face-to-face networking, online networking is quite limited, reinforcing the belief that the online environment will not replace the face-to-face one. Technology can be used as a filter to screen out unsuitable interactions and facilitate those that are valuable, but there's a magic that comes from connecting face-to-face that is almost impossible to emulate online.

Matchmaking software won't change this dynamic. Face-to-face meetings will still be essential. The equivalent of Tinder for events will only accelerate the creation of the right connections, both during events themselves and over the course of the entire year.

People who don't have access to effective matchmaking technology may leave shows disappointed that they haven't met the right people. Justifiably, they may blame the organizers for that scenario. Unless they are completely unreasonable, however, they will never blame event organizers for their own failure to close deals. It's the job of organizers to create an environment that maximizes connection and enables people to meet the people they want to meet. Matchmaking software will certainly play a role in allowing that role to be fulfilled more effectively.

The technology that allows people to meet is already available. The challenge for the events industry is to harness the different aspects of that technology into the creation of a coherent whole. This is an extremely exciting facet of event tech, and it illustrates the best elements of the junction between face-to-face and digital. When digital technology is used to enhance the experience and the productivity of participants in face-to-face events, everyone can benefit.

SENSOR-DRIVEN DATA MAPS INTERACTIONS WITH EXTRAORDINARY ACCURACY

Never in human history has it been so easy to know where people are and what they're doing. Sensor-driven mobile technologies allow event attendees to monitor the movements of others in an accurate yet unobtrusive fashion. It's possible, for example, to know who has recently checked into an event, where they are situated, and what specific conferences and meetings they are participating in.

That information makes it much, much easier to determine which meetings, sessions, or cocktail parties are the most likely to yield valuable connections. To facilitate this dynamic even further, some venues have installed beacons that transmit signals from Bluetooth devices, revealing the whereabouts of their users. Others are utilizing inexpensive near-field communication (NFC) technology for the same purpose.

Heat maps track movement around sporting events, trade shows, and conferences, providing information such as how many people there are in a specific aisle or area of the venue. Similar to radar maps on the Weather Channel, varying concentrations of people show up as different colors on heat maps. Red indicates a large volume of people, yellow a middling number, and green a small number.

Heat maps provide both organizers and exhibitors with insight into the most desirable locations for booths, opening up the possibility of variable pricing. This model is already in use at shopping centers and malls, where stores pay more to rent the most valuable locations. Another advantage of knowing where people are is that new services can be created based on this information. Buyers or sellers may be willing to pay to have personalized text messages dispatched to people they're interested in connecting with, precisely when those people are nearby.

As discussed earlier in this chapter, events generate a lot of data. Yet, the face-to-face industry is still in the early stages of understanding how best to capture and use that data. It should be possible to build an app that allows event attendees to read the moods of other participants, making it easier to calibrate conversations.

Within a few years, it's likely that event organizers will track the movements of everyone attending their shows. They will be able to assess the various meetings that take place and extrapolate the information they collect onto relationship graphs. These graphs will deliver useful information, such as the percentage of people meeting those they have previously connected with via social networks and the percentage with no previous online connection. It will also be possible to determine *which* social networks are the most effective for facilitating connections.

This information could be used to build better shows for everyone. It will be easier to ascertain whether specific attendees are likely to benefit from particular shows based on their history of relating with other attendees. For attendees with few previous connections, it will be possible to provide additional tools and orientation to help them make the most of their participation and want to return.

Geolocation technologies that are already used in shopping malls, theme parks, and hotels enable those with access to the data to gain significant insights into user behavior. Some of these technologies are becoming so mature that they may soon be able to track indoor activity—within exhibition centers, for example—without beacons or NFC technologies. Understanding the behavioral patterns of event attendees is becoming easier and more affordable, and the technologies themselves continue to improve. This represents another huge opportunity for the events industry to combine the power of data capture with the unique quality of face-to-face interaction to strengthen and evolve the events landscape.

EVENT MANAGEMENT SUITES MAKE INTEGRATING TECHNOLOGY EASIER

For people whose businesses depend on face-to-face connections, the prospect of focusing a lot of energy on technological innovations may seem daunting. As technology improves, however, companies are springing up with a specific remit to handle the technological needs of events.

Cvent is one example. The company handles registration, data capture and analysis, marketing, matchmaking, and the management of relevant mobile apps, among other services. Etouches and Lanyon operate in the same vein.

This level of integration is still not easy to achieve, but there are several start-ups striving to make it easier.

With so many different companies racing to integrate event technology more smoothly, it's still not clear who will succeed. What's certain is that it will happen, and probably soon. There is no doubt that all the problems we have described could be resolved, or at least significantly improved, by the appropriate use of existing technologies, but that's not the point. Successful tech players in many industries have created amazing software applications, but those solutions have not been designed specifically for the live events industry.

The dynamics and specific needs of live events require deep customization and integration among many existing players. For the first time, we are starting to see bright entrepreneurs partnering with smart investors and organizers, working together to fix these problems. It bears repeating that these are still very early days, but the speed of change is accelerating and the early successes of many of these young companies are quite impressive.

HARNESSING THE POTENTIAL OF DIGITAL SPONSORSHIP

Imagine that you're organizing a seventy-thousand-person trade show for the luxury travel industry. Who will participate? Attendees will certainly be wealthy. What products will they be interested in?

Event organizers are starting to realize that if they collect data about the people who come to their events, they can use it to present sponsorship as a valuable opportunity. For example, some event organizers may be able to demonstrate that there are three million people in the United States who come to their events and that those people are interested in banking services or luxury cars. That information makes brands such as BMW and UBS possible sponsors.

At present, most of the business-to-business industry is yet to see the value of selling sponsorships, but that's beginning to shift. As the knowledge of what's possible spreads through the industry, it's probable that sponsorship will become a much more widely used tool. In addition, sponsorship offerings will become more diverse, as sponsors see the value of reaching out to the existing audiences of shows. They may look to sponsor the production of newsletters, for example, instead of focusing only on shows.

What exactly is an e-product? For some companies, it can be as simple as a sponsored post on Facebook or Instagram. For others, it may mean providing a digital event bag. If you've ever attended a show, you've probably had the experience of receiving a "goody bag" full of material related to the show. These swag bags are opportunities for sponsors to engage in branding and deliver messages to attendees.

Unsurprisingly, not every participant chooses to collect one of these bags. They are often heavy and uncomfortable to carry around all day. Many event organizers are already considering reducing the amount of paper they provide at events. One solution is to offer everything that would normally be provided in physical form as a "digital goody bag." By putting all the information and branding on a website, it remains easily accessible.

Like the newspaper industry, the events industry is still very much in transition between the predigital age and an era in which digital integration will become commonplace in every aspect of our lives and businesses. The comparison is instructive. At first, consuming news digitally was seen as an additional service for those who already subscribed to physical newspapers. Many people still see digital technology in that light: as an auxiliary component of a primarily physical offering, not a separate business.

That perception, however, is slowly changing. People in the events industry are gradually coming to understand that digital technologies have the ability to reshape the entire ecosystem. The hope, naturally, is that face-to-face events prove more resilient than newsprint and more capable of finding business models that support digital innovations, while growing, as opposed to diminishing, the industry's core offerings.

OTHER TECHNOLOGIES

As described earlier in this chapter, high numbers of smartphones, tablets, and computers inside conference rooms are contributing to distracted audiences. It's not uncommon to see as many as 80 percent of participants in a given session more engaged in checking their messages, texting, or reading news on their iPads than on the material being presented. This phenomenon creates huge challenges for speakers, which may ironically be solved most effectively by using technology.

XP Touch is user-engagement software that allows presenters to interact with audiences via their electronic devices. This means that attendees can follow sessions *using* their smartphones and tablets, instead of being distracted by them. The software also allows speakers to boost interaction by conducting polls and votes and asking questions. Similar to XP Touch, Slido is an audience-interaction tool, designed to make presentations more engaging. It integrates with mobile apps and other tools, and allows users to lead question-and-answer sessions, conduct votes and polls, and share presentations.

Twitter is another tool that has already found a foothold in the face-to-face industry. Twitter walls have become a very popular way to gauge attendee response and create a sense of community, as an experience shared among attendees is broadcast to the world.

A third innovation is CrowdMics, which allows users to transform their smartphones into microphones. You probably have the experience of waiting while microphones are set up, moved, or tested before a talk. It's likely you also sat patiently while a single mic was transported around the room during a question-and-answer session. CrowdMics puts an end to the awkwardness of that situation by allowing everyone in the audience—and, at a pinch, on stage—to turn their phones into their own personal microphones.

Technology is an inescapable presence in all our lives. Used badly, it's a considerable threat to the ability to be focused and present. Used well, however, the reverse is true. Tools such as CrowdMics, Slido, and XP Touch enlist technology itself in the fight against distraction.

HOW WILL FACE-TO-FACE EVOLVE?

There's nothing inherently *wrong* with the format of face-to-face events. It's simply human nature to become distracted. The problem is that most event organizers have not yet fully embraced the potential of technology or started to see it as an ally. When people don't have the tools to make the most of their experiences at events, they turn their attention to smartphones and tablets. Technology is fascinating. Never in human history have we had access to so much information accessible at the tap of a finger or through voice-activated assistants.

It's the job of everyone in the industry to ensure that we counter technology that distracts with technology that engages. Perhaps no industry has yet truly managed the transition from analog to digital. Models are emerging all the time: some work and thrive; others fail and die.

Earlier in this chapter, we discussed the newspaper industry, an example of a field where the move from analog to digital has been anything but smooth. Physical newspaper sales are falling, but customers are still unwilling to pay for digital news. The face-to-face industry is in a much better position than many other ecosystems to ride the wave of change and emerge stronger. The core offering of connecting with the right people at the right time is inherently valuable. In a digital world, the personal connection this engenders is perhaps even more precious.

While the face-to-face industry will not die, there is a possibility that it will fail to evolve quickly enough and disappoint the people who should be its biggest supporters. Consumer expectation is a powerful force, and people who are used to a high level of digital integration in other areas of their lives will not respond well to a perceived lag on the part of the events industry.

Jochen Witt, however, sees reason for optimism. Witt is the president and CEO of JWC, a management consultancy firm specializing in trade fairs and related areas. He says that "We definitely believe that organizers are ready to embrace new technologies." The variable in his estimation is the *type* of technology. "When it comes to visitor registration and floor planning, many organizers are fairly advanced, or at least have a clear strategy. Areas many organizers are struggling with is what technology to use for data mining, digital offerings 24-7, and even onsite matchmaking."

As this chapter has shown, those areas offer some of the greatest opportunities, if only they can be harnessed. In the next chapter, we'll look more closely at some other industries and ask how they are meeting the challenges of technological change.

CHAPTER THREE

LESSONS FROM OTHER INDUSTRIES

———

Received wisdom states that the media revolution is a recent phenomenon. In reality, however, it has been building for many years. We're currently in a period of massive transition for media as a whole. The days in which everyone picked up one of the same few newspapers in the morning and watched one of the same few TV shows in the evening are long gone. The Internet and Netflix have seen to that.

Many other industries are experiencing far more serious disruption than the face-to-face events field, and have even more profound questions to answer about their places in a world of new technology. On the other hand, some have begun to come to terms with the shift and are starting to flourish in this new ecosystem. In this chapter, we'll take a look at how the lessons from other industries apply to the face-to-face landscape and how they can help people in the events industry prepare for the next phase.

The period of change usually commences when technologies become affordable, scalable, and predictable. This is already the case in the news and television industries. In the face-to-face industry, we are on the verge of seeing this shift take place. Once change takes hold, it will continue to affect the industry for many years because the technology continues to change and improve at such a rapid pace. Upcoming generations of customers, users, and investors, who have grown up with technology and feel very comfortable making it an integral part of their daily lives, will fuel those changes with their enthusiasm for adopting new improvements.

Anybody who tells you that they know exactly how this is going to happen is lying or delusional. Even the world's most sophisticated media players are humble enough to recognize that the scope of change is currently beyond their understanding. They don't know exactly where it will take the industry, and they can't be sure which industry categories will experience the greatest disruption. No one should doubt, however, that established industries can and will be disrupted.

Nevertheless, the vast majority of our interviews with some of the most successful and sophisticated executives and entrepreneurs in the events industry revealed similar convictions. Very few believed that a disruptor on the scale of Uber or Airbnb was likely to land in the events space. Instead, most anticipated "category disruptors," technologies that will shift some *part* of the face-to-face industry. Eventbrite is a perfect example of a category disruptor. The company made it much easier for companies to create attractive websites for their events and to handle registration online, but had no impact at all on facilitating better connections once participants actually *reached* events.

With so many different areas ripe for improvement and new technologies entering the space on a weekly basis, the arena is extremely crowded. This makes it highly competitive and very confusing for event organizers, sponsors, and visitors. For the next few years, this congestion is to be expected. It's a natural process that will sort the best ideas from the mediocre ones and gradually lead to the emergence of new industry standards. While there is still a long way to go, the initial phases of change are clearly visible. If you type "event technology" into a database of start-ups such as Crunchbase or Angel.co, you will discover hundreds of companies that have raised early-stage capital. Pretty soon, that number will be in the thousands.

Some of those projects will find traction and become successful, emulating Eventbrite, Cvent, and DoubleDutch. Once the most valuable technological developments have been selected, the industry will begin to stabilize and reach a state of maturity.

The newspaper industry has already been severely disrupted by digital technology. The same is true of magazines, television, and the music industry. Laptops and smartphones have radically altered the way people consume media of all kinds. Young people watch TV on their phones, iPads, and laptops. Instead of relying on centralized broadcast channels, they subscribe to services such as Hulu, Netflix, and HBO NOW. Billions of dollars that were previously spent on the services of traditional cable operators are now directed toward streaming platforms.

Despite these manifold changes, the television industry continues to grow. Digital technology hasn't killed it. Some other media channels are struggling more intensely. Many newspapers, for example, have been forced to shift their business models completely, from relying on sales of paper copies to seeking digital subscribers and generating entirely new revenue streams. Some of these are founded on digital innovation and now represent significant segments of their businesses. Many people, your authors included, believe that a similar process could play out in the live events industry and that in a relatively short period of time—ten years or less—digital revenues will have a significant role to play in the live events industry.

The nature of the Internet, based as it is on the free exchange of information, has sometimes made this difficult, a situation compounded by the billions of dollars newspapers have lost in classified advertising revenue. Online players such as Craigslist allow people to post ads for nothing and reach many more people than the traditional classified ad. As a result, many news media outlets are finding the shift from paper to digital hard to pull off.

The music industry is similarly in flux, although it seems to be weathering the storm more effectively than the news media industry. Sales of CDs have dropped through the floor, replaced by online subscriptions to streaming services such as Spotify and direct purchases from iTunes and Google Play. The music industry was quick to pursue legislation against players such as Napster that made copyrighted material available at no charge, with the result that labels have retained some level of control over the process of digitization. Nonetheless, there's been a definite shift of ownership from the labels toward the artists.

Prior to widespread digital technology, it was necessary to visit a store in order to sample and purchase a given product. Now, it's easy to make purchases online. Reviews, ratings, and information about pricing are also easily accessible online, making it possible to compare retailers and make a decision from the comfort of home. Shopping online saves time, money, and stress in comparison with shopping at stores.

Even though there are huge advantages to shopping online, malls have not simply disappeared. They have adapted their business models, embracing technology to improve customer experience and make shopping more fun. In many ways, retail mirrors the face-to-face industry here. Every technology described in this book has been tested or used in some capacity by the retail industry.

Retail shares a number of similarities with the face-to-face industry. Technology is a threat to traditional retail businesses, but they can capitalize on the fact that the satisfaction of human interaction is not available online. Brick-and-mortar retail players rely on the business of people who do their research online but transact offline. This offline element of the process opens up a whole new world of data, presenting new possibilities and solutions.

Until recently, there was no way to easily map traffic in a retail environment or to know how long people spent looking at particular products. A lot of digital retail technology is focused on questions such as these, helping retailers make informed decisions about where to locate items, cash registers, and assistants. They no longer need to rely on guesswork. Now they have data.

Like the face-to-face industry, the retail industry is still in the early phases of this transition. Nonetheless, it can already boast some excellent technologies. Most of these advancements are data-centric. They allow retailers to track customer behavior and connect those customers with items they may be interested in. Some retailers are using messaging to alert people to offers they may like or to the locations of stores with sales.

One start-up, CloudTags, integrates online and offline experiences by enabling customers to learn more about in-store products using their smartphones and tablets. It also facilitates the creation of the offline equivalent of a shopping cart. Prior to CloudTags, there was no way to follow up with customers who considered making a purchase in-store but ultimately decided against it. Now, retailers have a method of tracking the interests of patrons and reconnecting with them.

All these technologies have applications for the events industry. Broadly speaking, any innovation that allows event organizers to create a more personalized experience for attendees, sponsors, and exhibitors has value in the face-to-face field. Another parallel is the world of automobile insurance, where telematics is now allowing insurers to assess actual driver behavior. This new data allows insurers to craft new, fairer business models. In the past, good drivers often paid more than they needed to for car insurance because it was difficult to divine patterns from large quantities of aggregated data. Telematics enables insurers to determine premiums based on actual driving habits, not broad, demographic-based numbers.

This principle applies to events just as much as to automobile insurance. The success of events is based on what people do when they're there, not merely on indicators such as number of attendees. In the past, the tools allowing for insights into attendee behavior were few and relatively crude. Event organizers relied on paper surveys and employee feedback to gauge participant satisfaction.

Technological innovations promise to shed light on user behavior in ways that could only have been dreamed of before the dawn of the digital age. New technologies will make it possible to glean direct insights into what makes for a good show, as opposed to relying on a combination of intuition and hope.

As we converse with entrepreneurs in the growing fields of retail and marketing technology, it is clear that there is huge potential for everyone in these related specialties to learn from one another. As described earlier, we believe the most successful and disruptive solutions for the face-to-face industry will come from outsiders, at least initially. Those who are not embedded in the events industry will be able to bring fresh eyes to industry problems and resolve them more effectively than those whose established ways of thinking blind them to innovative solutions.

WHAT DRIVES PEOPLE TO CONNECT FACE-TO-FACE?

There are three key drivers motivating conference and trade show participants. The first is efficiency. Buyers and visitors attend events to research new products, services, and technologies and often to purchase them at big discounts. Two days at a show represents an excellent investment of time for people who will have the opportunity to explore potential purchases in a highly condensed time frame.

The second driver is education. Attendees want to collect new information that is relevant to their specific businesses, confer with industry experts and peers, and learn about the overall state of the industry. The third and final driver is networking. An event is an effective way of meeting many people in a short space of time. In the past, it was not always easy to orchestrate a succession of meetings. It was hard to even know in advance who was attending the event. As a result, meeting the right people was largely a matter of chance. In theory, social platforms such as Facebook and LinkedIn make it easier to ascertain who will be attending a given event ahead of time. This method is still a bit hit or miss, however.

It's possible to make gains in efficiency, education, and networking without venturing to an event. Online platforms make it easy to conduct research, products can be traded online, and platforms such as TED.com or FORA. tv make it easy to consume content from the comfort of home. Nonetheless, the crux of this book is that as yet, the online experience simply cannot replace the face-to-face one. Relationships between vendors and buyers are forged over several years and are based on mutual trust. A good partnership is more than simply a transactional experience. It consists of a friendship built on shared experience and an emotional bond. This is not an easy commodity to replicate online.

There is a joke in the events industry that goes, "Until it's possible to get pregnant online, the face-to-face industry will remain relevant." It's tempting to take a doomsday approach to technological change, bemoaning the way it disrupts an industry many of us have worked in for decades, but it's a lot more productive to realize that nothing can replace the experience of meeting face-to-face and to ask how technology can *improve* the events industry.

Here's a theoretical example. Imagine that you are a plastics engineer traveling to Germany for a conference. A few months prior to the conference, you receive an e-mail from the organizers with information about keynote speakers. The organizers are already creating an environment in which you will feel motivated to attend the event and listen to what the speakers have to say. Following the event, you want to review the talks given by the speakers. Your notes were quite vague, and you feel sure that you missed an essential point relating to your field of expertise. Is the content lost forever? It needn't be. If the organizers are on the ball, they should be making content available to attendees after or even during the event via live streaming.

Access to online content is practically free and virtually unlimited. Anyone who can use Google can find a treasure trove of relevant content online. This makes it essential that content producers and event organizers provide added value. They are competing with a plethora of online content options. The downside of this superabundance of content, however, is that each online content provider is in the same situation. They are all competing against one another for a portion of our limited attention spans.

TED Talks, for example, are free and provide a huge amount of interesting content. Their very accessibility, however, is also their limitation. Precisely *because* they are available anywhere, at any time, it is hard for most people to commit to them. Succumbing to distraction is a constant temptation. Compare this experience with the experiences of those who attend TED conferences live. Sitting in the same hall as the speaker and sharing an unrepeatable moment with a unique combination of other people is a rare experience for most of us. That makes it precious and shapes the way we interact with the event.

People who attend TED Talks live have invested time and money to be present. They are more likely to make the most of that investment than people who have simply switched on an online video. They are also more likely to be open to meeting new people, discovering new products, and doing business. Passive consumption of online content encourages a correspondingly passive mindset. An active approach to attending an event nourishes an active, engaged attitude to the experience of participation.

EMBRACING TECHNOLOGY IN THE FACE-TO-FACE INDUSTRY

The in-person experience is still irreplaceable and will only get better as technology intervenes to resolve some of the frustrations typical of face-to-face events. In five years' time, events will be considerably more productive, and investments will yield improved returns.

For hundreds of years, the events industry has sold space in broadly the same way. A floor plan is used to determine the locations of each booth or stand, and each exhibitor is charged the same flat fee. As described in chapter two, heat maps and traffic density technologies are becoming realities. Event organizers are starting to make use of the data they provide to create a tiered pricing model, charging exhibitors based on the popularity of particular locations.

This is helping exhibitors that benefit from high levels of traffic maximize their returns on investment. Conversely, it's also helping specialized exhibitors that don't require a high level of casual foot traffic. They can save money and trust that the people they really need to meet will find them. Over the course of the business year, this may make it more affordable for some smaller exhibitors to participate in more events.

Jochen Witt is already seeing organizers that "provide distinctly different business models to their customers." Instead of selling exhibition space, they "provide matchmaking to their customers on the basis of sophisticated technology." Witt is aware that this business model may not be applicable to many events, but, he says, "It is very well suited to serve niche industries or niche events."

Conference organizers can learn from retailers. Technology is creating a better experience for shoppers, attracting people to stores through combining the lure of face-to-face interactions with some of the benefits of online shopping. This is precisely the task facing the in-person events industry: to take the best of what is available digitally and integrate it into an improved face-to-face experience.

Event attendees want to capture more and better information, and to seal more business deals during the time they spend at events. When they attend keynote speeches, they want speakers to share information in a more engaging way. Once they leave events and return home, they want to access valuable content from the conference. Exhibitors want to capture more detailed and accurate data about attendees, both before and during events. They want to use that data to connect with the right potential clients and to keep in touch with those clients throughout the year. Digital technology offers event organizers an outlet to satisfy the needs of both attendees and exhibitors.

The role of an event organizer is a complex one. Organizers work with visitors, exhibitors, sponsors, and speakers, all of whom have different needs. When all these partners embrace new technologies, the return on investment grows for everyone. This only happens, however, when there is buy-in from all sides. It isn't enough for event organizers alone to embrace digital technology. Events consist of numerous stakeholders, and no significant change will take place until new norms are established.

Part of the job of modern organizers is convincing each of these stakeholders to accept and embrace technological developments, because only when everyone involved is willing to explore the opportunities offered by digital innovation will those opportunities truly manifest. Imagine that you are a savvy event organizer and have selected a mobile app with which to communicate with your speakers, exhibitors, and attendees. What will happen if they are not also using the app? Right: nothing. Facebook's colossal power consists in its vast number of users. If it ceased to be a useful tool for connecting, it would quickly go the way of other failed social networks. The same is true for any new technology in the face-to-face ecosystem. Its success depends on market penetration.

Event organizers are responsible for creating successful events, so they are the right people to spearhead the uptake of useful new innovations. A good event organizer today should be looking to uncover valuable technologies and *share* them with other stakeholders. Their engagement is the key to turning a good idea into a positive reality. This approach is very easy to discuss in a book or mention in a conference, but extremely difficult to execute effectively. It requires a serious commitment of time and energy on the part of event organizers and a willingness on the part of attendees, exhibitors, and speakers to adopt new ideas and become their advocates. Some organizers are making a considerable effort, only to meet with indifference or resistance from other stakeholders. This attitude will not foster progress. Anyone truly interested in ushering in the age of digital technology must understand that this is an active partnership involving everyone in the industry.

A BONFIRE AROUND WHICH TO MEET

The changes already described in this book are merely the tip of the iceberg. Eventbrite has changed perceptions of what's possible in the arena of event registration, but that doesn't mean it's the final word on the subject. The Holy Grail, as discussed in chapter two, is the creation of a "Tinder for events" application that facilitates connections between buyers and sellers.

Another two areas offering great potential for innovation are virtual reality (VR) and augmented or mixed reality (AR/MR). The former is becoming mainstream: Google's new Daydream headset is a big step up from the company's previous offering, Cardboard. Facebook, too, has a presence in the market with the Oculus brand. VR headsets create a simulated immersive environment, and they're growing rapidly in popularity. In theory, there's no reason why VR couldn't make it possible for people all over the world to experience events without being physically present. AR technology allows users to project objects from their phones and mobile platforms in the form of holograms. It's still very new, but we believe that AR/MR companies such as Magic Leap will have a big impact on the events industry.

By 2016, Magic Leap succeeded in raising $1.4 billion of investment capital, and the company is working on its product, to be launched within a year or two. This level of valuation and investment in the VR/AR/MR sector reflects investor appetite for the technologies and the view that it is potentially a massive market—both business-to-customer and business-to-business—that should generate attractive profits.

We believe—and time will tell whether we are right or wrong—that VR/AR/MR could and should impact the live events industry in a big way. We already see smart entrepreneurs working on different use cases that can generate very interesting opportunities—and challenges—for event organizers.

Salim Ismail of Singularity University says that we're living in a world where we're either the disruptor or the disrupted. In a talk about exponential technologies, he discusses the capacity of tech giants such as Apple and Google to tackle almost any problem they choose, using small, highly focused teams.[9] This dynamic is equally applicable to the world of event tech.

The smartphone in your pocket is a thousand times more powerful than the computer that put a man on the moon. This exponential acceleration of technology already provides us with a huge amount of information, which is only increasing. All this change can seem scary indeed. It's tempting to shy away from it and wish for a return to more stable and predictable days. What seems like a crisis, however, can also be an amazing opportunity to create better events.

For centuries, the face-to-face industry has helped people around the world earn a living and grow their businesses. That's a record to be proud of. Nonetheless, we cannot live

9   http://videos.singularityu.org/category/exponential-technologies/

in the past. Already, the changes we have seen over the past decade have been more profound than the changes the industry witnessed over the previous 850-plus years of its existence. The coming decade will usher in even greater change and even greater opportunity.

However large the changes, the basic goal of the face-to-face industry will remain intact. Bob Priest-Heck is the president of Freeman, a family-owned company with an eighty-eight-year history. Freeman organizes more than 15,000 events and live experiences each year. During a conversation with your authors, Priest-Heck made the following comment:

> Sometime in the Stone Age, people decided that it was a good idea to gather around a bonfire and eat, exchange bits of wisdom, and see what the other hominids knew about hunting, healing and finding a reliable source of food and shelter. The invention of smoke signals, wall painting, printing presses, telegraphy, telephones, and emoji may have changed how we connect, but not the basic need to connect. People consistently tell us they like to connect face-to-face, and many invest the time and money to travel even when the convention and expo content is offered online. There is true value in what our industry offers—a bonfire around which to meet face-to-face.

Digital technology is not a means of dousing that bonfire. It's a way of fueling it.

CHAPTER FOUR

MAGICAL OPPORTUNITIES

———

Many of the changes we have analyzed in this book will generate fantastic opportunities for the face-to-face industry. Undoubtedly, the journey will not always be a smooth one. At times, the ride will be very bumpy. Some companies that are currently very successful will struggle to survive. Some events with long histories will fail to adapt to the changes. There are events all over the world that have been running for more than fifty years and yet are beginning to decline because some sponsors and exhibitors prefer new and different business models.

In Europe, centuries-old companies and long-established events are dramatically altering such models. They understand that change is inevitable and all parties involved with live events are eager to test new models. In the United States, growth predictions for the trade show industry in 2017 are hovering around 3 percent. Meanwhile, digital revenues related to live events are growing by more than 25 percent a year.

By applying simple math to those numbers, it becomes obvious that billions of event dollars will soon be shifting from one established business model to an as-yet-uncertain "something else." Embracing these challenges, understanding potential trends, and being brave enough to engage with the cycle of testing/learning/fixing/retesting is part of a key cultural change that the industry is starting to realize is critical to future success, perhaps even survival.

The greatest fear for event organizers is that someone else will come along and master the technology before they do. For any brand that relies on capturing the attendance of hundreds or thousands of people, disruption by a new player in the industry has the potential to prove cataclysmic.

In the words of Bob Priest-Heck, however:

Let's say that the second biggest risk in our industry is investing in technology or digital innovations that don't pan out. The bigger risk is always going to be complacency: a fear of risk. That's why I don't worry about what the competition is doing; I worry about what we're *not* doing. We're looking to grow by attracting the "digital generation," who experience a lot of their young lives through "the rectangle." [We want] to introduce them to a whole new world of live experiences that can be enhanced by their love of technology to create a new medium. We want to offer them better, richer, limitless experiences.

Modern consumers are becoming ever more demanding. A few years ago, they may have been content to passively consume technological change. Now, they expect event organizers to adapt to changes in the market and are willing to go elsewhere if their needs aren't served.

We've discussed the consequences of being afraid of this dynamic at length. Suffice to say, we're convinced that inaction and denial are a far more dangerous strategy than learning how to embrace and utilize new technology to the advantage of everyone in the industry. Magical opportunities will only occur if we are willing to greet technological shifts and the positive changes they bring with a resounding "yes." They give us tools with which to maximize engagement and satisfaction and gain valuable insights into the behavior of potential partners.

While the landscape may appear more confusing and unpredictable as old certainties are swept away, that unpredictability can also look like opportunity. No longer do a few big players control technological innovation. Anyone in the face-to-face industry who is prepared to seize control of their destiny will soon have the tools to do so. Every innovation we've discussed in this book can be perceived negatively, as an unwelcome change, or positively, as a powerful opportunity. The more we can focus on the latter, the better shape we'll be in.

In chapter two, we discussed the fact that the majority of event attendees now make use of smartphones and tablets while they are in the conference room. This can be a disruptive and distracting dynamic, or it can be a huge opportunity to engage audiences in conversation via mobile apps.

The key is not to fight the natural human tendency toward distraction but instead to channel it. The television industry is already providing an example of how this can be done. HGTV, along with other networks, is actively encouraging viewers to connect with certain TV shows via their phones. This interaction supports the programs they are watching on their televisions.

Another example is retail. Think about all the times you have visited clothing stores and tried on shirts, only to leave without making a purchase. Every time that happens, a huge amount of information about your preferences is not captured. Why didn't you buy the shirt? Did you decide you didn't like the color? Was the shirt too big or too small? Did you feel it was too expensive? Perhaps you were simply distracted by another task before you were able to find the right shirt.

Imagine that instead of leaving the store without making a purchase, you had a device that allowed you to interact with each item of clothing in a store in the same way you can on a website. It would be possible to save the shirt for later purchase or explore the availability of different sizes and colors. Instead of giving up and visiting a different store, you would be much more likely to research your options and follow through with some kind of commitment. Technology in the events industry can have a similar impact. Rather than thinking of digital technology as a form of competition for the current state of the industry, we can think of it as a complementary new channel that augments the overall experience of everyone in the face-to-face ecosystem.

Perhaps the most potent existing example of what may be possible is the advent of Amazon Go. This service allows customers to swipe their phones when they enter a store, take what they want, and leave without passing through a checkout. Their phones automatically register their purchases, which are charged to their Amazon account.[10]

The democratization of technology is both unnerving and a powerful opportunity. Historically, large companies controlled the manufacture and usage of the best tools because they were the only organizations that could afford to develop and manufacture those tools. Now, everyone in the industry has access to incredibly potent tools. In the world of e-commerce, large, costly infrastructure frameworks are no longer required. Any small business can create a digital storefront that is just as appealing as any large competitor's.

This dynamic has yet to fully take hold in the events world, but there are numerous examples from other industries that demonstrate what may be possible. Consider Meetup. This website makes it possible for anyone to organize meetings, anywhere, with practically no technical knowledge. It makes messaging an entire group of people simple and straightforward. In short, it has made connecting with like-minded people considerably easier, quicker, and safer.

10   https://www.youtube.com/watch?v=NrmMk1Myrxc

Blogging software is another example of a technological development that has changed how we perceive the world. The launch of blogging software made it simple for writers to publish their thoughts, using a pleasant, user-friendly interface. The emergence of blogging software coincided with the proliferation of search engines such as Google, meaning that unknown bloggers suddenly had an avenue for promoting their work and developing a readership. Blogging democratized the publication of opinions and information, a field in which there were traditionally high barriers to entry.

Existing technologies such as blogging and Twitter are increasingly valuable as methods of generating additional content and community engagement for live events, even when their impact is not immediately obvious. The use of hashtags, for example, may seem like a very minor development. Certainly, it would be hard to argue that hashtags are creating disruption in any meaningful way, but they are providing event attendees with a way of sharing their experiences and photos, and connecting with other people who have also shared content. This improves the event experience for participants and provides organizers with an easy way to gauge the mood of their audiences.

Many event organizers have already started commissioning mobile apps that are relevant specifically to their events. Typically, these apps are installed for the duration of a particular show and subsequently deleted. They are very useful for attendees but have no application beyond a very short period. The creation of a mobile experience that stretches throughout the year represents another potential magical opportunity for the face-to-face industry.

If this magical opportunity is to be grasped, however, the next generation of creators must be inspired and supported to create solutions. The technology and use cases for mobile solutions for live events already exist. They are growing fast, and we fully expect to be surprised by amazing smartphone applications with specific utility for concerts, sports, trade shows, conferences, and many other live event experiences.

Smartphones are not going away any time soon, and their power, versatility, and capabilities will continue to grow. Smart entrepreneurs will be able to figure out new and creative ways to use these handheld supercomputers and to create a better, more engaging, fun, and productive event experience.

Mobile opportunities will merge with new technologies such as VR/AR/MR and create completely new ways for people to interact within and around live events. These engagement opportunities may be face-to-face or digital—live streaming—or both. We constantly receive pitches from very smart people with fantastic concepts, and we are confident that many of these ideas will become multimillion-dollar companies in the near future.

While some venture capitalists are already starting to recognize the potential of the $565 billion events industry, this potential remains largely untapped. There are signs, however, that change is on the move. Pandora recently acquired Ticketfly for $450 million. While it's still too soon to tell whether this move heralds a sea change, it could be a good sign.

As David Audrain, executive director of the Society of Independent Show Organizers, notes, "The priority for event organizers continues to be the same as it has always been, to bring the right buyers and sellers together. If a technology can be proven to make that process more efficient or effective, it is likely to get their attention."

WHAT IS AN EVENTS COMPANY ANYWAY?

In Europe, especially in Germany, a single entity controls events, venues, and vendors. Some people love this model, and others hate it. In the early days of the PC era, Apple chose to create value by controlling every aspect of their users' experience, whereas Microsoft chose to provide a universal operating system. Today, the same dynamic is playing out in the smartphone market. Android is adopting the same approach as Microsoft did in its early days and has captured a tremendous market share by taking an inclusive approach. Some might argue, however, that Apple has been more successful by keeping a tight rein on both its products and operating systems.

A similar conversation plays out in the world of events. Some players want to control everything, from the venue to the content to the distribution channels. In an era of technological democratization and year-round connectivity, however, is it even possible to exercise that level of control? When events are no longer simply three- or four-day experiences, who will own them? How will the face-to-face industry bridge the gap between the offline and online communities? Will it work better to create a proprietary experience, or to collaborate broadly and trust the unpredictability of connections as they multiply? It may be twenty years before we can give a definitive answer to these questions, and many companies will fall and others will rise in the process. As an industry, however, we must be brave enough to embrace these experiments and use them to power the industry into the coming decades.

Event organizers recognize that some communities like to gather more frequently than once or twice per year and to keep in touch through consuming and discussing content online. In some cases, they are also creating small, casual, in-person gatherings that complement larger and more traditional face-to-face events. Brands seeking to serve these diffuse communities must be able to connect with them via a range of both online and offline touch points, not only through huge one-off shows.

There are two primary approaches to serving communities of this type. The first is ideals driven; the second is deals driven. The ideals-driven approach tends to appeal to millennials, who often operate from a desire for pure knowledge about what is best for themselves and others. They are eager to stand for something. The best way to serve people who are ideals driven is through year-round engagement. This engagement needn't be sophisticated, but it should include the provision of valuable content and the opportunity to network as part of a digital community. This could mean daily interaction via a discussion group or weekly engagement via content consumed in a newsletter. It could also mean casual in-person meetings once a month, supplemented by larger, more traditional events every quarter or six months.

Conversely, the deals-driven approach is more transactional. Business-to-business (B2B) is a huge part of the global trade-show business, and trade and transactions—not necessarily *at* an event, but certainly in its aftermath, as meetings and research come to fruition—are a critical component of success. The important question to be addressed is how technology is helping—or hindering—these potential transactions. After decades of trial and error, we are finally seeing successful B2B online marketplaces generate real traction. Are these marketplaces the enemy, or are they a potentially powerful partner for trade shows? The jury is still out. As you might imagine, this is a question that generates strong responses from many players in the industry, who are debating whether they should build their own platforms, buy those that already exist, or set up in partnership with these new digital B2B players.

As the activities of event organizers change, everyone in the events industry is forced to consider what exactly constitutes an events company. Are events the same things they always have been, or are they evolving into something entirely new? Technology is altering the very definition of what constitutes an event and an events company.

We recently heard a fascinating conversation between two leading event organizers, who asked the following question: "Should event organizers be digital companies who happen to organize live events or will we continue to be event organizers who happen to apply digital tools?"

Very smart live events people are starting to realize that digital disruption could be as big as it was around print, music, or TV, and are investing tons of money and resources trying to figure out potential trends and new revenue opportunities that could have a material impact on their businesses.

In the print domain, Time Warner made the mistake of thinking it was in the magazine business, when in reality it was a content company. In the same way, event organizers must realize they are not strictly defined by the fact that they run event companies. Their wider remit is to serve the industry as a whole by facilitating relationships. The more they focus on the qualities that make their work valuable, the more magical opportunities they will create. Flexible definitions make it easier to embrace changes and perceive them as an opportunity to experiment.

The events industry must avoid making the same mistakes as the print industry, which put a stake in the ground and bred an "us versus the world" mentality. If event organizers try to operate on a territorial basis, they will see that territory vanishing from beneath their feet. If they choose instead to see the shifting terrain as an opportunity to take leaps, they will surely find that the digital age offers many magical opportunities.

As Denzil Rankine puts it, "Data has been ignored [until now], and too many decisions are based on gut feel. Winning organizers are no longer sales led; they have marketing and data at the core."

CONCLUSION

CAUSE FOR EXCITEMENT

———

At a recent conference in Europe, your authors spoke to an audience of about five hundred event organizers. When we asked how many of them entered this industry by accident, about 99 percent raised their hands. Marco had a very similar experience.

As a twenty-two-year-old marketing director for Apple in Latin America, part of his job was to attend events in San Francisco, Europe, and elsewhere. He was always excited by the vibrancy of those events and the connections he made. A pivotal moment came at his first MacWorld Expo in 1992. (Yes, he's quite old!) At that event, he met exhibitors who marveled that they had done enough business in two days to boost their results for an entire year. Others told him that what they had learned at the expo would significantly alter the way they structured their businesses.

Marco left the venue to take a walk and pondered what he had heard. As he walked, he realized what a powerful marketing tool events could be. When run well, they were an incredibly effective way of helping a tremendous number of people take huge strides in a very short time. As an Apple employee, he was already passionate about technology. He left that MacWorld Expo nurturing a new passion: events.

Eventually, Marco left Apple and founded his own small events company, which later grew into a multimillion-dollar business. He sold that company to Reed Elsevier, the largest event organizer in the world. During this period, he also cofounded two other companies focused on media and the Internet, and experienced the fun and adrenaline that comes from taking a simple idea and turning it into a company ready to sell to strategic buyers willing and able to take it to the next level.

In 2008, Marco founded Vesuvio Ventures, in homage to his Italian roots and his passion for the beauty of southern Italy. The company was primarily an excuse to invest money and time in working with both amazing entrepreneurs and large companies, while making a genuine effort to connect with startups and nurture innovation in a pragmatic and productive fashion. Marco gives presentations about changing the way people connect, do business, have fun, and enjoy events, media, and technology, a role that brings him into contact with some very smart people who are working on large and complex problems.

Marco also presents specific use cases and examples that tackle the questions of how big corporations can work and innovate in partnership with startups, and how early-stage companies can benefit from corporate partnerships, during their early days, to accelerate growth and maximize success. This book is an attempt to organize some of the fruits of those conversations into a single document, to be used as a resource by anyone with an interest in the events industry.

Marco and Jay connected through a mutual friend, who recommended Jay's expertise in lead generation and advertising tech to Marco. That was the start of a wonderful friendship and a productive partnership.

Prior to working with Marco, Jay was a domain expert. He attended a lot of events, but none of them felt like a true fit for his personality and interests. There were aspects of each he related to, but there were always elements with which he didn't connect. In 2005, he was invited to speak at an event for the first time. Although it was an overwhelming and nerve-wracking experience, he loved the rush that came with preparing material and delivering it in front of an audience, and soon committed to speaking at more events. Before speaking at one particular conference, he searched the itinerary for any mention of his field of expertise, lead generation. Among fifteen categories, there was not one mention of lead generation to be found. Jay suddenly realized that the events industry was not set up to cater to people like himself and felt highly motivated to create events for those who shared his interests.

Neither Marco nor Jay trained formally to enter the face-to-face events industry. There's a good reason for this: There *is* no formal training for entering the face-to-face industry. It is interesting, and a trifle concerning, that such a large industry is not served directly by a single academic institution. The face-to-face events industry is not considered a valid subject of study by a single credible university on the planet, so there is no direct path for talented event organizers or technological entrepreneurs to follow. Currently, most people with an interest in events learn by joining big players in the industry and picking up knowledge and wisdom as they go.

This will surely change. The events industry is changing rapidly, and it's doubtful that a traditional academic course could effectively serve the needs of those who have an interest in entering the industry. It's more likely that education for the industry will evolve to become intensive and interdisciplinary, covering the varied skills and talents required to succeed in the field.

Trevor Foley, managing director of tfconnect, points out that the question is changing from "How do we modernize?" to "Who do we need to have within our business in order to modernize?" In November 2015, Foley asked a community of senior human resources professionals in the digital industry for their positions on a range of topics relating to hiring, retention, and training in the events sphere.

More than 73 percent strongly agreed that there is an urgent need for people with better digital skills and experience in the industry. Not a single person disagreed. In the same survey, 90 percent valued digital experience at least as highly as events experience in senior marketing professionals. Only 18 percent said that it was difficult for them to justify hiring digital experts who didn't have previous knowledge of events.

There is no doubt that the live events industry stands in great need of new skill sets and management capabilities.

Every single company that organizes or participates in events recognizes that the classic method of participation is no longer valid. We hear regularly that event organizers are looking to hire data analysts, digital marketers, full stack developers, and many other people with talents that were not in demand a couple of years ago. Almost every large or medium-sized event organization company already employs people as chief digital managers and in similar roles. This is only the first expression of the search to meet a completely new set of needs and embrace the challenges and opportunities described in this book.

An interesting analogy can be drawn with computer coding. People are learning to code in nontraditional settings, such as boot camps, and the education is aimed not at providing them with a qualification but at preparing them for a job. As a result, people are learning quickly. They don't need academic degrees. They need the skills that make them valuable to employers.

However education for the face-to-face industry evolves, your authors want to see people *choosing* live events as a career path. It's important that the industry send a message that face-to-face events are powerful and will only become more powerful as digital technology is integrated into the events ecosystem. The industry must present itself as an attractive and exciting career choice, encompassing diverse disciplines from technology to human behavior and psychology.

Both Marco and Jay have spent time engaging with strong and well-respected academic institutions in the United States, Europe, and around the world, all of which are exploring the question of how best to educate the next generation of face-to-face event organizers. They have seen a great deal of knowledge and talent employed in service of these initiatives and, more importantly, a well-spring of enthusiasm from smart, talented young people eager to learn about the world of events.

A FINAL WORD

As this book draws to a close, it's important to emphasize that the events landscape is changing so rapidly and dramatically that knowledge from even five years ago is becoming less relevant. The only way to future-proof the industry is for those who care about it to continue exercising their curiosity and always keep learning. Those who are not curious about how the industry can become better may find that they are left behind while it moves onward without them. This is also why companies, start-ups, executives, and entrepreneurs must be fully engaged in the education of their teams and the support of educational initiatives.

Ultimately, the face-to-face industry is about people. Organizers who wish to succeed must think about the best ways to serve exhibitors, speakers, and attendees, arranging the agenda, the floor layout, and even the bar in a way that maximizes their enjoyment and satisfaction. For those who are interested in marketing and like to understand human psychology, events are an excellent environment in which to develop those interests.

The metrics for success in the events industry are changing. Some years ago, success was measured in terms of how many square feet of floor space event organizers could sell. The industry was all about hitting the right numbers. This is all changing. Ten years from now, square feet will no longer be considered an adequate measurement of success. As with so many aspects of this fast-changing field, we don't yet know precisely what metrics will replace square feet. The key is that we identify them early and ensure that they are relevant.

The face-to-face industry is currently in the midst of an identity crisis. As with all crises, it brings the opportunity to emerge stronger and more unified. We want to see it make a transition that enables it to remain important for the next 850 years.

Working in the events industry is like an addiction. If you like it, it's extremely difficult to leave. If not, it's hard to stay for two hours. The pressure, speed, and need to hit deadlines can be brutal, which repels some people and attracts others. Those of us who love it wouldn't trade the excitement and adrenaline of a good event for anything.

David Adler, founder and CEO of BizBash, makes a poignant point: "Event organizers," he says, "are among the most courageous people I know. After listening to Brené Brown's TED Talk on vulnerability and courage, it occurred to me that hosting an event of any type is putting all your vulnerability out on the table. It opens all the organizers to judgments, criticisms, and every possible thing that could go wrong."

As Theodore Roosevelt famously opined, "It is not the critic who counts; not the man who points out how the strong man stumbles, or where the doer of deeds could have done them better. The credit belongs to the man who is actually in the arena."

Event organization of all types encompasses not only being in the arena but also creating the entire venue. Face-to-face experiences change lives. Your life could be changed by a concert you find deeply moving, a live sports experience that cements the bond between you and your family, or a trade show that enables you to meet challenging and ambitious business goals. In each of these cases, technology is your friend, not your enemy. It is a method for improving the traditional in-person experience.

This is why both Marco and Jay are so excited to be part of the events and event-tech industry. We may be living in challenging times, and the future may be uncertain, but if we choose to embrace change, great things are on the horizon. It's an exciting time to be part of the face-to-face industry, and will only become more exciting.

APPENDIX

SUPPORTING DATA

——

GLOBAL INTERNET USAGE
CONTINUE TO GROW
EXPONENTIALLY.

Global Internet Users, 2008-2015

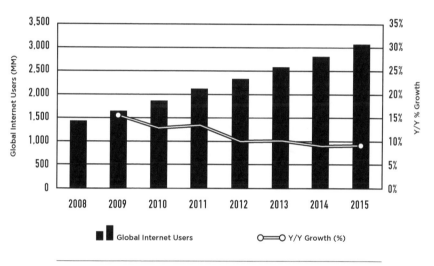

SOURCE: United Nations / International Telecommunications Union, US Census Bureau. Internet user details as of mid-year. Internet user data for China from CNNIC, Iran from Isalamic Republic News Agency, citing data released by the National Internet Development Center, India from IAMAL, Indonesia from APJII/eMarketer.

WE HAVE REACHED
A CRITICAL MASS OF
SMARTPHONE ADOPTION.

Smartphone Users, Global, 2005-2015

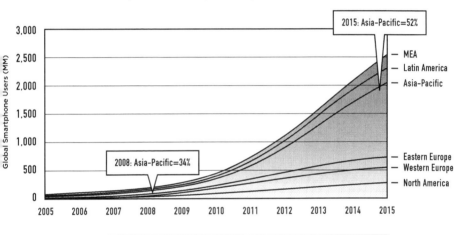

SOURCE: Nakono Research (2/16). Smartphone users represented by installed base.

THE NUMBER OF NEW
COMPANIES FOUNDED TO
BRING ENTREPRENEURS INTO
EVENT TECH IS GROWING.

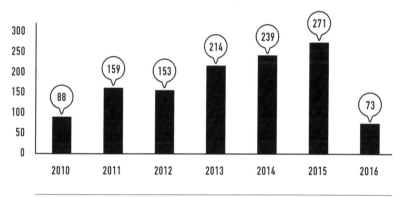

YoY — Number of companies founded

SOURCE: Tracxn Technologies Private LTD. (2016).

SOME OF THE MOST RELEVANT
LARGE CATEGORIES AROUND
LIVE EVENTS (WITH MANY
MORE COMING SOON).

Large Upcoming Sectors

No. of Companies Founded	Average Age	No. of Companies Funded	Business Model	Total Funding	Example
35	Jan. 2015	4	Ticketing > Consumer > Listing Platform > Local Event Discovery	$797k	NoddApp 2015, Mumbai
16	Sep. 2014	2	Ticketing > Consumer > Listing Platform > Local Event Discovery > Nightlife	$650k	Goyano 2015, Delhi
57	Nov. 2013	17	Planning > Organizer Tools > Artists > Marketplace	$2m	Bookya 2014, Kuala Lumpur
68	Aug. 2013	14	Planning > Organizer Tools > Vendor > Marketplace	$32m	Eved 2010, Chicago
16	May 2013	7	Planning > Organizer Tools > Sponsorship Platforms	$3m	SponsorHub 2010, New York City
25	Feb. 2013	8	Ticketing > Consumer > Marketplace > Primary > Local Event Discovery > Nightlife	$2m	Akrass 2015, Tel Aviv
19	Jan. 2013	1	Planning > Organizer Tools > Venue > Discovery > Listing Platform	$202k	Elite Meetings 2006, Santa Barbara

SOURCE: Tracxn Technologies Private LTD, (2016).

SOME OF THE MOST RELEVANT
LARGE CATEGORIES AROUND
LIVE EVENTS (WITH MANY
MORE COMING SOON).

Large Upcoming Sectors

No. of Companies Founded	Average Age	No. of Companies Funded	Business Model	Total Funding	Example
111	Nov. 2012	34	Planning > Organizer Tools > Venue > Discovery > Marketplace	$151m	Convene 2009, New York City
23	Aug. 2012	14	Ticketing > Consumer > Marketplace > Crowdfunding	$14m	MyMusicTaste 2011, Seoul
121	Jun. 2012	38	Ticketing > Consumer > Listing Platform > Horizontal	$65m	Everfest 2015, Austin
21	Jun. 2012	2	Planning > Organizer Tools > Vendor > Listing Platform	$4m	Celebrations.com 2008, New York City
114	Feb. 2012	49	Ticketing > Consumer > Marketplace > Primary > Local Event Discovery	$1.2b	Sash SF 2010, San Francisco
32	Sep. 2011	10	Attendee Engagement > Audience Interaction	$9m	Beekast 2014, Paris
49	Jun. 2011	18	Attendee Engagement > Networking	$55m	nTAG Interactive 2002, Austin

SOURCE: Tracxn Technologies Private LTD, (2016).

SOME OF THE MOST RELEVANT
NICHE SECTORS AROUND
LIVE EVENTS (WHICH ARE
GROWING EXPONENTIALLY).

Niche Upcoming Sectors

No. of Companies Founded	Average Age	No. of Companies Funded	Business Model	Total Funding	Example
10	Nov. 2012	5	Ticketing > Consumer > Marketplace > Primary > Sports	$4m	Shoowin 2016, New York City
3	Aug. 2012	1	Ticketing > Consumer > Marketplace > Primary > Local Event Discovery > Experiences	$25m	IfOnly 2011, San Francisco
4	Jun. 2012	3	Marketing > Promotion > Digital Media > Referral	$13m	StreetTeam 2012, London
15	Jun. 2012	8	Ticketing > Consumer > Marketplace > Primary > Concerts	$32m	Dice 2016, Ottawa
10	Feb. 2012	6	Ticketing > Consumer > Listing Platform > Sports > Marathons	$12m	Mala App 2009, Beijing
6	Sep. 2011	2	Attendee Engagement > Live Campaign Management > Event App > Events	$27m	Osmosis 2015, Seattle
15	Jun. 2011	10	Marketing > Promotion	$25m	Invite The Media 2015, Paris

SOURCE: Tracxn Technologies Private LTD, (2016).

SOME OF THE MOST RELEVANT
NICHE SECTORS AROUND
LIVE EVENTS (WHICH ARE
GROWING EXPONENTIALLY).

Niche Upcoming Sectors

No. of Companies Founded	Average Age	No. of Companies Funded	Business Model	Total Funding	Example
3	Jan. 2012	3	Marketing > Personalized Marketing > Experiential Marketing	$18m	Event Farm 2010, California City
2	Jan. 2012	2	Marketing > Suite	$2m	Feathr 2011 Gainesville
13	Nov. 2011	4	Marketing > Lead Generation > Event Data	$3m	RainFocus 2012, Lindon
13	Jul. 2011	10	Marketing > Promotion > Digital Media	$25m	SpinGo 2012, Draper
3	Aug. 2010	2	Ticketing > Consumer > Marketplace > Re-Pricing	$110m	ScoreBig 2009, Los Angeles
15	Jun. 2010	6	Attendee Engagement > Audience Interaction > Feedback Tools	$1m	PigeonLab Pte Ltd. 2010 Singapore
4	Feb. 2010	2	Planning > Organizer Tools > Venue > Layout Management	$23m	Social Tables 2011, Wash. D.C.

SOURCE: Tracxn Technologies Private LTD. (2016).

SOME OF THE MAJOR
ACQUISITIONS IN THE LIVE
EVENT SPACE IN THE 2016
CALENDAR YEAR. LARGE DEALS
ARE FINALLY HAPPENING
IN THE EVENT TECH SPACE,
AND MANY MORE WILL BE
COMING ON THE HORIZON.

Major Acquisitions in last one year

Date	Company	Acquirer	Deal Size	Overview	Funding
Nov. 2016	Cvent Fairfax, 1999	Vistaequity partners.com	$1.65b	Insight Venture Partners, NEA, Greenspring Assoc., Birchmere Ventures, CTW Venture Partners	$154m
Jul. 2016	Mtime Beijing, 2005	wandacinemas.com	$350m	Movie review, information, merchandise and ticket selling platform Draper Fisher Jurvestson, Tiger Global Management, CBC Capital, Fidelity Growth Partners, Aslo, Eight Roads Ventures, Wanda Cinemas	$14m
May 2016	Ticketbiz Madrid, 2009	ebayinc.com	$165m	Secondary Ticketing Marketplace Active Venture Partners, Fabrice Grinda, Fil Rouge Capital	$17m
Jun. 2016	Flavorus Los Angeles, 1999	vivendi.com	$4m	Ticketing marketplace and software provider	
Oct. 2016	YPlanApp London, 2012	timeout.com	$2m	Ticketing platform—Qualcomm Ventures, General Catalyst Partners, Nokia Growth Partners, Wellington Partners, A-Grade Investments, Octopus Investments, Slow Ventures	$37.7m
Dec. 2016	Cinepapaya Lima, 2012	fandango.com	Undisclosed	Online and mobile sales of movie and festival tickets Start-Up Chile, 500 Startups, Mowile, Wayra	$2.55m
Sep. 2016	Attend.com Boston, 2013	eventfarm.com	Undisclosed	Event Management and Engagement Platform, forermerly Attendware, 405 Ventures, Comerica	$6.6m

SOURCE: Tracxn Technologies Private LTD, (2016).

THE SPEED THAT COMPUTERS, CELL PHONES, AND THE INTERNET HAVE BEEN ADOPTED OUTPACE ALMOST ALL PREVIOUS TECHNOLOGIES.

Technology adoption, (1900-2005)

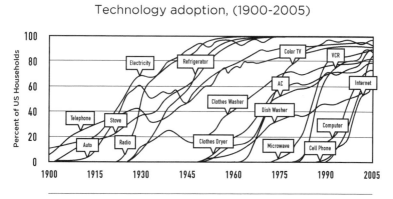

SOURCE: Michael Felton, *The New York Times*

THE SPEED OF COMPUTER
PROCESSORS HAS GROWN
EXPONENTIALLY FOR THE
PAST 100 YEARS.

Exponential growth of computing for 110 years

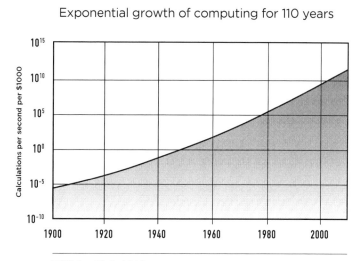

SOURCE: Kurzweil, *The Singularity Is Near.*

A HIGHER AND HIGHER
PERCENTAGE OF THE WORLD'S
POPULATION IS USING THE
INTERNET EVERY DECADE.

Global population and Internet users (2000-2020)

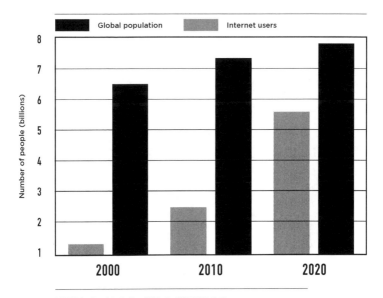

SOURCE: http://www.futuretimeline.net/21stcentury/2020-2029.htm#ref3.

MOBILE SUBSCRIPTION
GROWTH HAS BEEN STEADY
IN BOTH THE DEVELOPED AND
THE DEVELOPING WORLD.

Mobile Cellular Subscription Growth (2000-2010)

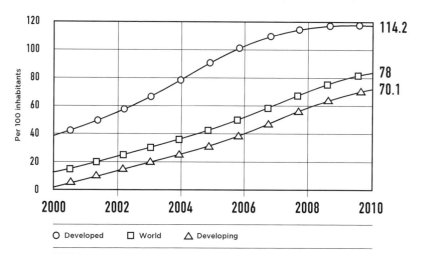

O Developed   □ World   △ Developing

SOURCE: http://www.itu.int/ITU-D/ict/publications/idi/2011/Material/MIS_2011_without_annex_5.pdf;
http://www.itu.int/ITU-D/ict/publications/idi/2010/Material/MIS_2010_without_annex_4-e.pdf.

TOTAL BANDWIDTH GROWTH HAS
INCREASED EXPONENTIALLY
IN BOTH THE DEVELOPED AND
THE DEVELOPING WORLD.

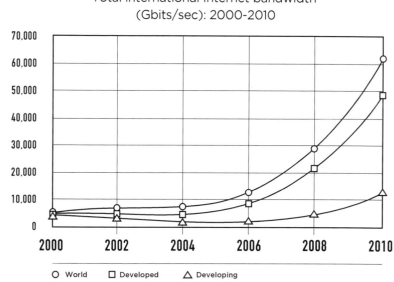

Total international Internet bandwidth
(Gbits/sec): 2000-2010

O World   □ Developed   △ Developing

SOURCE: http://www.itu.int/ITU-D/ict/publications/idi/2011/Material/MIS_2011_without_annex_5.pdf;
http://www.itu.int/ITU-D/ict/publications/idi/2010/Material/MIS_2010_without_annex_4-e.pdf.

ABOUT THE AUTHORS

 **JAY WEINTRAUB** is the founder and CEO of NextCustomer, a business-to-business events incubator whose portfolio consists of Grow.co and Contact.io. He is a graduate of the University of Pennsylvania.

 **MARCO GIBERTI** is a successful entrepreneur and angel investor with more than twenty-five years of intensive experience in marketing and communications with focus on the media, Internet, and events industry.

47159008R00106

Made in the USA
Middletown, DE
18 August 2017